WHOLLY SANCTIFIED

Wholly Sanctified

Living a Life Empowered
by the Holy Spirit

A.B. SIMPSON

CHRISTIAN PUBLICATIONS
CAMP HILL, PENNSYLVANIA

Christian Publications
3825 Hartzdale Drive, Camp Hill, PA 17011
www.cpi-horizon.com

Faithful, biblical publishing since 1883

ISBN: 0-87509-455-4
LOC Catalog Card Number: 91-71132
© 1991 by Christian Publications
All rights reserved
Printed in the United States of America

98 99 00 01 02 7 6 5 4 3

CONTENTS

Preface

This volume is a classic appeal for true holiness and purity of heart by a master in the spiritual life, and it is for all those in every generation who hunger and thirst after righteousness.

In this revised edition of Dr. A.B. Simpson's widely accepted work on sanctification, the emphasis remains upon the possibility of each believer's experiencing perfect love through perfect faith and union with the Lord Jesus Christ. Dr. Simpson experienced and taught that "love is made complete among us . . . because in this world we are like him" (1 John 4:17), and that the full reception of our oneness with Jesus gives us perfect love.

Dr. Simpson's unique ministries to the body of Christ began well over a century ago. He served pastorates in Canada, Kentucky and New York before founding The Christian and Missionary Alliance in 1887. The warmth and vigor of his preaching, teaching and writing still come sharply into focus through his books, hymns and messages long after his death and promotion to glory in 1919.

Dr. Alfred C. Snead, one of Dr. Simpson's associates, when secretary for foreign missions in The Christian and Missionary Alliance, said of this volume:

Dr. Simpson has, under God's rich anointing, made clear to all who will read it in simple expectancy of faith in Christ, not only the essential character of the commandment to be holy, but also the way by which man may be enabled by the Holy Spirit to enter into God's purpose and know the reality of *Christ in you the hope of glory.*

If we who are elders in the Church of God, laborers in the vineyard of the Master, members together in Christ, would but live wholly sanctified lives, every problem which confronts, vexes, and often hinders the Church at home and in the mission fields would easily be solved.

I think that there are great numbers of Christian men and women who long daily for the fragrance of the Risen and victorious Christ in their lives. I commend this volume to them for Dr. Simpson makes it very plain that it is the full realization of our oneness with Jesus that gives us perfect love.

Dr. Louis L. King, president
The Christian and Missionary Alliance
(1978–1987)

CHAPTER 1

Wholly Sanctified

The prominence given to the subject of Christian life and holiness is one of the signs of our times and of the coming of the Lord Jesus. No thoughtful person can have failed to observe the turning of the attention of Christians to this subject along with the revival of the doctrine of the Lord's personal and premillennial coming. The very opposition which these two subjects have received and the deep prejudice with which they are frequently met emphasize more fully the force with which they are impressing themselves on the mind of our generation and the heart of the Church of God.

A clear illustration of this fact can be seen in a weathervane. The only way we can often know the direction of the weathervane is by the force of the wind. The stronger the wind blows against it, the more steadily does it point in the true direction. The very gales of controversy indicate more forcibly the intense interest with which the hearts of God's people are reaching out for a higher and deeper life in Him, and are somehow feeling the approach of a crisis in the age in which we live.

These two truths—holy living and Christ's Second Coming—are linked closely together in First Thessalonians 5:23–24. The former is the preparation for the latter, and the latter the complement of the former. Let us turn our attention, in prayerful dependence upon God and careful discrimination, to the explicit teaching of this passage respecting the scriptural doctrine of sanctification. May the Holy Spirit so lead and sanctify us both in our thoughts and spirits that we will see light in His light clearly and our prejudices will melt away before the exceeding grace of Christ and the heavenly beauty of holiness.

The Author of sanctification

The name, *God of peace*, implies that it is useless to look for sanctification until we have become reconciled to God and have learned to know Him as the God of peace. A justification so thoroughly accepted as to banish all doubt and fear and make God to us *the very God of peace* is indispensable to any real or abiding experience of sanctification.

Beloved, is this perhaps the secret cause of your failure in reaching the higher experience for which you long? "When the foundations are being destroyed,/ what can the righteous do?" (Psalm 11:3). Are there loose stones and radical difficulties in the superstructure of your spiritual life, and is it necessary for you to lay again the solid foundations of faith in the simple Word of Christ and the finished work of redemption? Then do so at once! Accept without feeling, without question, in full assurance of faith, the simple promises, "Whoever believes in the Son has eternal life" (John 3:36) and " . . . whoever comes to me I will never drive away" (John 6:37). Then take your stand on the Rock of Ages and begin to build the temple of holiness.

The expression *the very God of Peace* further suggests that sanctification is the pathway to a deeper peace, even the "peace of God, which transcends all understanding" (Philippians 4:7). Justification brings us peace *with* God; sanctification, the peace of God. The cause of all our unrest is sin.

> But the wicked are like the tossing sea,
>   which cannot rest,
>   whose waves cast up mire and mud.
> "There is no peace," says my God, "for the
>   wicked." (Isaiah 57:20–21)

On the other hand, however,

> Great peace have they who love your law,
>   and nothing can make them stumble.
>   (Psalm 119:165)

So we find God bewailing His people's disobedience and saying,

If only you had paid attention to my
  commands,
     your peace would have been
      like a river,
    your righteousness like the waves
      of the sea. (Isaiah 48:18)

Sanctification brings the soul into harmony with God and the laws of the soul's own being. There must be peace; there can be in no other way. Sanctification brings into the spirit the abiding presence of the very God of peace Himself. True peace is then nothing less than the deep, divine tranquility of His own eternal calm.

The deeper meaning of the passage is that sanctification is the work of God Himself. The literal translation of this phrase would be *the God of peace Himself sanctify you wholly.* It expresses in the most emphatic way His own direct personality as the Author of our sanctification. It is not the work of man nor means, nor of our own strugglings, but His own prerogative. It is the gift of the Holy Ghost, the fruit of the Spirit, the grace of the Lord Jesus Christ, the prepared inheritance of all who will enter in, the great obtainment of faith, not the attainment of works. It is divine holiness, not human self-improvement or perfection. It is the inflow into man's being of the life and purity of the infinite, eternal and Holy One, bringing His own perfection and working out in us His own will.

How easy, how spontaneous, how delightful this heavenly way of holiness! Surely it is a "highway" and not the low way of man's vain and fruit-less mortification. It is God's great elevated rail-way, sweeping over the heads of the struggling throngs who toil along the lower pavement when they might be borne along on His ascension path-way, by His own Almighty impulse. It is God's great elevator, carrying us up to the higher cham-bers of His palace without our laborious efforts, while others struggle up the winding stairs and faint by the way. It is God's great tidal wave bear-ing up the stranded ship until she floats above the bar without straining timbers or struggling sea-men, instead of the ineffectual and toilsome efforts of the struggling crew and the strain of the en-gines, which had tried in vain to move her an inch until that heavenly impulse lifted her by its own attraction. It is God's great law of gravitation lift-ing up, by the way of sunbeams, a mighty iceberg that a million men could not raise a single inch, but that melts away before the warmth of the sun-shine and rises in clouds of evaporation to meet its embrace until that cold and heavy mass is floating in fleecy clouds of glory in the blue ocean of the sky.

How easy all this! How mighty! How simple! How divine! Beloved, have you come into the di-vine way of holiness? If you have, how your heart must swell with gratitude as it echoes the truths of the words you have just read! If you have not, do you not long for it and will you not now unite in the prayer of our text that the very God of peace will sanctify you wholly?

The nature of sanctification

What does *sanctify* mean? Is there any better way of ascertaining than tracing its scriptural usage? We find it employed in three distinct and most impressive scenes in the Old Testament.

Sanctify means to separate. This idea can be traced all through its use in connection with the ceremonial ordinances. The idea of separation is first suggested in the account of creation in the first chapter of Genesis, and there, probably, we see the essential figure of sanctification. God's first work in bringing order, law and light out of chaos was to separate, to put an expanse or gulf between the two worlds of darkness and light, of earth and heaven. He did not annihilate the darkness, but He separated it from the light, He separated the land from the water, He separated the waters of the sea from the vapors of the sky.

We see Him in the spiritual realm, immediately afterwards, separating His people. He separated the family of Seth from the worldly race of Cain. He separated Noah and his family from the ungodly world. He separated Abraham and his seed from an idolatrous family. He separated Israel from Egypt and the surrounding nations. The very meaning of the word church is *called out or separated.* To each individual the same call comes still,

"Therefore come out from them
    and be separate,
            says the Lord.

Touch no unclean thing,
   and I will receive you."
"I will be a Father to you,
   and you will be my sons and daughters,
         says the Lord Almighty"
Since we have these promises, dear friends,
let us purify ourselves from everything that
contaminates body and spirit, perfecting holiness out of reverence for God. (2 Corinthians 6:17–7:1)

Sanctification then means our voluntary separation from evil. It is not the extinction of evil. It is
the putting off, the laying aside of evil by the de-
taching of ourselves from it and placing an impass-
able gulf between us and it. We are to separate
ourselves not only from our past sins but from sin
as a principle of life. We are not to try to improve
and gradually ameliorate our unholy condition.
We are to put off the old life, acting as if it were no
longer ourself, and separating it from our sinful
self as the wife is divorced from her husband, and
as the soul is separated from the body by death.
We are to reckon ourselves dead indeed unto sin
just as much as though we were no longer the
same person, and the old heart was no longer that
true self (see Romans 6:11).

We are to refuse every manifestation of evil,
whether from within or from without; every sug-
gestion and temptation; every impulse that is not
of God. We are to be in the attitude of negation
and resistance with our whole being saying no!

We need not annihilate the evil or resist it in our own strength but simply, by a definite act of will, separate ourselves from it, hand it over to God and renounce it utterly. Give Him the absolute right to deal with it and destroy it. When we do so, God always follows our committal with His almighty power and puts a gulf as deep as the bottomless grave of Christ and a wall as high as the foundations of the New Jerusalem between us and the evil we renounce.

We separate ourselves; God makes the separation good. The first decisive step in sanctification is an act of will by which we renounce evil in every form in which it is made manifest to our consciences and brought into the light. We deny further not only evil in its manifestations but also the whole evil self and sinful nature from which each separate act has sprung.

We also separate ourselves from the world and its embodiment of the old natural condition of things and the kingdom of the prince of evil. We recognize ourselves as not of the world even as He was not of the world. We put off, not merely that which is sinful, but that which is natural and human that it may die on the Cross of Jesus and rise into a supernatural and divine life. "Therefore, if anyone is in Christ, he is a new creation; the old has gone, the new has come" (2 Corinthians 5:17).

The Holy Spirit leads us to a deeper separation, not only from the evil but also from the earthly. He lifts us into a supernatural life in all respects, and prepares us, even here, for that great transformation in which "the perishable has been clothed with the imperishable, and the mortal with immortality" (1 Corinthians 15:54). For as the first man was of the earth, earthy, even before he fell, so will he give place to the second man who was made a living spirit and who has lifted us up into His own likeness.

The practical force

What then, is the practical force of this thought? As God shows you your old sinful self and every evil working of your own fallen nature, you are definitely to hand it over to Him, with the full consent of your will. He then will separate it from you and deliver you wholly from its power. You are to reckon it as being in His hands and no longer having control over you or in any sense belonging to you. As He leads you further to see things that might not be called sinful and yet are not incorporated into His life and will, you should separate yourself and surrender them to Him so that He may put to death all that is apart from Himself and raise up in a new and resurrection life our entire being.

You will see that you are delivered from the death struggle with evil and the irrepressible conflict with self. Your part will be simply to hand Agag over with your own hands for execution (see account in First Samuel 15), and gladly consent that the Lord should slay him utterly and blot out the remembrance of Amalek forever.

You must surrender

Beloved, have you thus separated yourself for God to sanctify? *Yours must be the surrender.* God will not put His hand on the evil until you authorize Him with your glad consent. Like Joab's army of old, He encamps before your city and sends you the message that Sheba must die or the city perish, but your own hands must deliver him over. Have you done so or will you do so? Will you not now with glad consent lay your hand upon the blessed Sin-Offering's head, and transfer your sinful heart and the dearest idol it has known, to Him who "made Him who had no sin to be sin for us, so that in him we might become the righteousness of God" (2 Corinthians 5:21).

Sanctify means to dedicate. It is not only to separate from but to separate to. The radical idea of the word is to be set apart to be the property of another. We offer ourselves to God for His absolute ownership, that He may possess us as His peculiar property, prepare us for His purpose and work out in us all His holy and perfect will. This is the meaning of the appeal made by Paul in the statement:

> Therefore, I urge you, brothers, in view of God's mercy, to offer your bodies as living sacrifices, holy and pleasing to God—which is your spiritual worship. (Romans 12:1)

This too is the meaning of those oft-repeated expressions where we are spoken of as God's peculiar people, which literally means, a people for a possession. This is the very ground on which the Scriptures appeal to us to walk in holiness, because we are not our own; we are bought with a price and should glorify God in our body which is God's (1 Corinthians 6:19–20).

It is true that God has bought us, but here again His infinite condescension refuses to compel our surrender, and will accept nothing but a voluntary gift. So, gladly constrained by love, we feel it a privilege to belong to Him and have Him stoop to take us in our worthlessness and be responsible for all the risks of our momentous existence.

This is what the term consecration properly means. It is the voluntary surrender or self-offering of the heart, by the constraint of love to be the Lord's. Its glad expression is, "I belong to my lover" (Song of Songs 7:10). It must spring, of course, from faith. There must be the full confidence that we are safe in this abandonment, that we are not falling over a precipice or surrendering ourselves to the hands of a judge, but that we are sinking into a Father's arms and stepping into an infinite inheritance.

It is an infinite privilege to be permitted to give ourselves up to One who pledges Himself to make us all that we would love to be—all that His infinite wisdom, power and love will delight to accomplish in us. It is the clay yielding itself to the potter's hands that it may be shaped into a vessel unto honor, and meet for the Master's use. It is the poor street waif consenting to become the child of a prince that he may be educated and provided for, that he may be prepared to inherit all the wealth of his guardian. How ashamed we may well feel that we ever hesitated to make such a surrender, or that we ever qualified it with any condition but His good and perfect will!

Beloved, have you made this full surrender? If so, how gladly our whole being says "Amen" to all that we have said of the blessedness of being only the Lord's! If not, let it be done this moment and at His feet of love prostrate yourself as a whole burnt offering and cry,

> Take my poor heart and let it be,
> Forever closed to all but Thee;
> Seal Thou my breast, and let me wear
> Thy pledge of love forever there.

Sanctify means to fill. The literal translation of the old Hebrew word to consecrate is "to fill the hand." It suggests the deepest truth in connection with sanctification, viz., that Christ Himself must be the substance and supply of our new spiritual life and fills us with His own Spirit and holiness.

After the most sincere consecration, we are but an empty possibility that He must make real. Even our consecration itself must look to Him for grace to make it faultless and acceptable. Our will must be purified and kept single and supremely fixed on Him, by His continual grace. Our purity must be the imparting of His life; our peace, His peace within us; our love, the love of God shed abroad in our hearts. Our very faith, which receives all His grace, must be continually supplied from His own Spirit.

He is the supply

We bring to Him but an empty hand, clean and open, and He fills it. We are a capacity; He is the supply. We give ourselves to Him fully, understanding that we do not pledge the strength or goodness required to meet our consecration, but that we take Him for all, and He takes us, fully recognizing the responsibility which He assumes to make us all that He requires and keep us in all His perfect will as we let Him through the habit of a full surrender. What an exquisite rest this gives to the trusting heart and what an infinite grace on His part to meet us on such terms and bear for us so vast a responsibility!

In the upper portion of New York City many citizens may often have noticed, especially in the past years, a great number of miserable shanties, standing on the choicest sites. Though perhaps on the corner of a splendid new avenue or looking out on a magnificent prospect, the house was utterly unworthy of the site. Suppose that a millionaire should want to purchase this site, and that the owner should begin, before giving possession, to repair the old shanty for the new owner, putting fresh thatch on the miserable roof and a new coat of whitewash on the dirty walls.

How the purchaser would laugh at him and say, "My friend, I do not want your miserable old wreck of a tenement fixed up like this. At the best it will only be a shanty when you have done all you can to it and I will never live in it. All I want is the ground, the site, and when I get it I will raze the old heap of rubbish to the foundations, and dig deep down to the solid rock before I build my splendid mansion. I will then build from the base my own new house according to my own magnificent plan. I do not want a vestige of your house, all that I require is the location."

This is exactly what God wants of us and waits to do in us. Each of us has a splendid site for a heavenly temple. It looks out upon eternity and commands a view of all that is glorious in the possibilities of existence. The house that is built upon it now, however, is a worthless wreck, it is past improving. Our patching and repairing is worse than waste. What God wants of us is simply that we give Him the possibilities of our lives and let Him build upon them a temple of holiness which He will make His own abode and which He will let us dwell in with Him as His happy guests in the house of the Lord forever.

From the very foundations, the work must all be new and divine. He is the Author and Finisher of our faith, and the true attitude of the consecrated heart is that of a constant yielding and constant receiving.

This last view of sanctification gives boundless scope to our spiritual progress. It is here that the gradual phase of sanctification comes in. Commencing with a complete separation from evil and dedication to God, it advances into all the fullness of Christ, and grows up to the measure of the stature of perfect manhood in Him, until every part of our beings and every part of our lives are filled with God and become a channel to receive, and a medium to reflect His grace and glory.

Beloved, have we learned this blessed significance of sanctification and taken God Himself as the fullness of our emptiness and fountain of our spiritual life? Then, indeed, we have entered upon an everlasting expansion and ascension, and forever more these blessed words will deepen and broaden in their boundless meaning:

> Thou of life the Fountain art,
>   Ever let me take of Thee;
> Spring Thou up within my heart,
>   Rise to all eternity.

CHAPTER 2

A Sanctified Spirit

Having seen the source and meaning of sanctification, let us next trace its sphere and extent. "I pray God to sanctify you through and through" is the meaning of First Thessalonians 5:23–24. Paul then specifies the threefold division of our human nature, the spirit, the soul and the body as respectively the subjects of this work of grace.

The Divine Trinity has its counterpart in human nature. There seems good ground to claim that this division is recognized in the Scriptures.

In the original account of man's creation the body is first distinctly mentioned—"the Lord God formed man from the dust of the ground." Then we have the soul and spirit clearly distinguished in the words which follow, "and breathed into his nostrils the breath of life, and man became a living being" (Genesis 2:7). We have first the breath of the Spirit of the Almighty imparted into man's higher being and then the physical principle constituting him a living soul.

Again in the account of our Lord's childhood we have the same division. "And Jesus grew in wisdom [intellectual or soul life] and stature [physical life], and in favor with God [spiritual life] and men [social life]" (Luke 2:52).

Again in First Corinthians 2, the Apostle Paul very clearly distinguishes between the soul and the spirit in man. The psychical man, that is, the soul man, he tells us,

> does not accept the things that come from the Spirit of God, for they are foolishness to him, and he cannot understand them, because they are spiritually discerned. The spiritual man makes judgments about all things. (1 Corinthians 2:14–15a)

The psychical man, therefore, is the man of the soul; the spiritual man is the man of quickened spirit. Notice in this passage that he begins with the spirit and gradually descends to the soul and body as the subjects of sanctification. This is quite instructive and significant.

The other day in speaking to our janitors they remarked, "We always work from the top story downward and end with the basement, and so we never go back over our finished work, or need to soil the floors that have been cleansed and completed." In God's great house, He too works from the top downward.

So it is in the growth of the tree. Let it add a thousand layers, you will find that not one is laid on from the outside but each of them has a separate growth from the innermost pith of the tree. The tree's life is from within.

So too, in the tabernacle of Exodus, the great symbol of spiritual truth, we find Jehovah beginning in the Holy of Holies in the Ark of the Covenant, and traveling outward until He has moved through the sanctuary with all its sacred vessels, and reached the external court, with its laver and altar of sacrifice.

Beautiful type of the work of sanctifying grace; the holy Shekinah of the divine spirit and the indwelling Christ in the innermost chamber of the spirit, and spreading their heavenly life and influence abroad through every part until they penetrate every faculty of the soul and every organ of the physical being with their transforming and consecrating power.

What is the Spirit?

In a word it may be said that it is the divine element in man, or perhaps more correctly, that which is cognizant of God. It is not the intellectual or mental or aesthetic or sensational part of man but the spiritual, the higher nature, that which recognizes and holds converse with the heavenly and divine.

The spirit is that in us which knows God. It directly and immediately is conscious of the divine presence and can hold fellowship with Him, hearing His voice, beholding His glory, receiving intuitively the impression of His touch and the convic-

tion of His will, understanding and worshiping
His character and attributes, speaking to Him in
the spirit and language of prayer and praise and
heavenly communion. It is also directly conscious
of the other world of evil spirits, and knows the
touch of the enemy as well as the voice of the
Shepherd.

*The spirit is that which recognizes the difference be-
tween right and wrong.* It loves the right and thinks,
discerns, chooses in harmony with righteousness.
It is the moral element in human nature. It is the
region where conscience speaks and reigns. It is
the seat of righteousness and purity and sanctity.
It is that which resembles God, the new man created in righteousness and true holiness after His
image. Everyone must be conscious of such an element in his being and feel that it is different from
the mere faculties of the understanding or the feelings of the heart.

*The spirit is that which chooses, purposes, determines
and thus practically decides the whole question of our action and obedience.* In short, it is the region of the
will, that mightiest impulse of human nature, that
almost-divine prerogative which God has shared
with man, His child, that very helm of life on
whose decision hang the whole issues of character
and destiny. What a momentous force it is, and
how essential that it be wholly sanctified! As it is,
or is not, sanctified, the life is one of obedience or
disobedience. When the will is right, and the
choice is fixed, and the eye is single, God recognizes the heart as true and pure. "For if the will-

ingness is there, the gift is acceptable according to what one has, not according to what he does not have" (2 Corinthians 8:12).

The spirit is that which trusts. Confidence is one of its attributes and exercises. It is the filial quality in the child of God which looks in the Father's face without a cloud, which lies upon His bosom without a fear, and puts its hand in His with the abandonment of childlike simplicity.

The spirit is that which loves God. It is not the human emotional love of which we speak, for that belongs to the lower nature of the soul and may be most fully developed in one whose spirit is still dead to God in trespasses and sins. It is that divine love which is the direct gift of the Holy Spirit and the true spring of all holiness and obedience: nothing less than the love of God shed abroad in the heart by the Holy Spirit; its appropriate sphere is the human heart.

The spirit is that which glorifies God. It makes His will and honor its supreme aim and loses itself in His glory. The very conception of such an aim is foreign to the human mind and can be only received by a spirit which has been born again and created in the divine image.

The spirit is that which enjoys God. It hungers for His presence and fellowship and finds its nourishment, its portion, its satisfaction, its inheritance in Himself as its all and in all.

This wonderful element of our human nature is subject to all the sensibilities and susceptibilities that we find in a coarser form in our physical life.

There are spiritual senses and organs just as real and intense as those of our physical frame. We find them distinctly recognized in the Scriptures. There is the sense of spiritual hearing:

> He who has an ear, let him hear what the Spirit says to the churches.
> (Revelation 2:11a)

> Blessed are your . . . ears because they hear. (Matthew 13:16)

> My sheep listen to my voice; I know them, and they follow me. (John 10:27)

There is the sense of vision.

> Your eyes will see the king in his beauty
> and view a land that stretches afar.
> (Isaiah 33:17)

> Let us fix our eyes on Jesus. (Hebrews 12:2a)

> . . . beholding as in a glass the glory of the Lord. (2 Corinthians 3:18a, KJV)

> You have eyes but fail to see. (Mark 8:18a)

> To open their eyes and turn them from darkness to light, and from the power of Satan to God. (Acts 26:18)

There is the sense of spiritual touch.

I press on to take hold [or, grasp with my hand] that for which Christ Jesus took hold of me. (Philippians 3:12)

And . . . to let the sick just touch the edge of his cloak, and all who touched him were healed. (Matthew 14:36)

There is the sense of taste.

The one who feeds on me will live because of me. (John 6:57b)

Taste and see that the Lord is good.
(Psalm 34:8a)
He who comes to me will never go hungry, and he who believes in me will never be thirsty. (John 6:35)

There is the sense of smell. Very definitely it is referred to in Isaiah 11:2–3,

And the spirit of the Lord shall rest upon him, . . . And shall make him of quick under-standing [smell or fragrance, in the Hebrew: to delight in the odors of] in the fear of the Lord.

The spirit is real subsistence. When separated from the body after death, it will have the same consciousness as when in life, and perhaps more intense powers of feeling, action and enjoyment.

Such is a brief view of this supreme endowment of our humanity, this upper chamber of the house of God, this higher nature received from our Creator, and lost, or, at least, degraded, defiled and buried through our sin and fall.

What is it for the spirit to be sanctified?

It is indispensable that the spirit be quickened into life. It is dead by nature. The work of regeneration quickens it into vitality as a newborn life, breathed, given from heaven as unto us in the first creation, as from the very lips of God. In one sense, the unregenerate soul is not spiritually alive. Its faculties are alive, its animal life is active, but spiritually it is dead in sin. When "sin entered the world through one man, and death through sin," (Romans 5:12) not only did man become subject to physical death but spiritual death reigned also.

Thank God for the grace of God revealed in the gift by grace. Jesus Christ has delivered us from the bondage of death and enables us to reign in life by His own sacrifice.

What is a sanctified spirit?

It is a spirit separated. Have you ever looked at the dark, cold ground in early spring, that which would chill and defile your fingers if you drew your hand through? Perhaps it was mixed with the manure of the barnyard and the crawling earthworms that burrowed in it. Yet, have you never seen growing out of that dark soil, a little plant or flower, with roots white as the driven snow, and leaf as delicate and petals as pure as a baby's dimpled cheek? It stood unstained, separated by its own nature and purity from the dirty soil that was all around it.

So the spirit born of God is separated in its own divine nature from its own self and the sinful heart. The very first step of sanctification is to recognize this separation and count ourselves no longer the same persons, but partakers of the divine nature, alive unto God as those who have been raised from the dead. As such we are to separate our spirits from all that is not of God—not only from sin but also from the world and from self and our whole old natural life. All our spiritual instincts, senses and organs are to be separated from evil and intuitively to turn away from even the touch and approach of temptation. We are to refuse to hear with our inward ear the stranger's voice, see with the spirit's eye the fascinating vision of temptation, touch in spiritual contact any unclean thing, taste even the forbidden joy. By the quick sense of smell we are also to recognize and turn from the unwholesome atmosphere, and, as evil of any kind is revealed to the spirit, to renounce evil and to ask God to separate it from our spirit and to put the gulf of His presence between the soul and the sin.

It also must be separated ever from the spirits of others, and indeed, from any human spirit that could control it apart from the will of God. All of the aspects of the spirit to which we have already referred must be separated. The higher consciousness that knows God must be separated from all other gods but Him. The moral senses that know right must separate from all wrong. The will must be separated from the choice or inclination of all but His will. The power of trust must be voluntarily separated from every thought of unbelief or distrust. The power to love must be wholly separated from forbidden love. The aim and motive must be separated from all that is not for His glory; the source of its pleasure must be purified and the spirit separated from all joy that is not in harmony with the joy of the Lord.

Is your spirit separated, cleansed and detached from everything that could defile or distract you from the will of God and life of holiness?

Sanctified spirit is dedicated

A sanctified spirit is a dedicated spirit. Its powers of apprehension are dedicated to know God and to count all things but loss for the excellency of the knowledge of Christ Jesus (Philippians 3:8). His Word is the object of its deepest study and meditation, and His attributes and His glory the theme of its most delightful contemplation. To know God, be filled with His Spirit, and be ever in His presence is its highest aim. Its will is dedicated to God. It chooses Him deliberately as its portion and its sovereign Lord, and delights to abandon itself to His entire possession and to His perfect will.

It is this element of a single heart and a supreme

choice of God which constitutes what the Scriptures call a perfect heart. Every moral sense in the sanctified spirit is dedicated to God. It chooses His standards of right and wrong and desires above all things to bear His image and be conformed to His nature.

Its power of trusting is dedicated. It is determined to trust God under any circumstances and, in spite of all feelings, as an act of will chooses to believe His Word notwithstanding every discouragement and temptation. A spirit that thus chooses God will be sustained by the very faith of God Himself imparted to it.

Its love is dedicated as is its power of loving. It chooses to love God supremely and to love all as God would have us to love, regarding every human being in the light of God and His will, and adjusting itself to every relationship in such a manner as to please God. It is dedicated to the glory of God. It accepts this and not the applause of men nor its own pleasing as the true end and purpose of life and lays itself a living sacrifice on His altar.

Further, it is dedicated to enjoy God. It chooses Him as its portion, its happiness, all and in all. It consents to find all its satisfaction in Him and Him alone, whether it be in the loss of every other channel of happiness or by His filling all the springs of life with Himself.

A dedicated spirit is thus wholly given to God, to know Him, to choose His will, to resemble His character, to trust His Word, to love Him su-

premely, to glorify Him only, to enjoy Him
wholly and to belong to Him utterly, unreservedly
and forever. All its senses, susceptibilities and ca-
pacities are dedicated to Him. It yields itself to
Him to be made by Him all that He would have it
to be and to have His perfect will wrought out by
it forever. It chooses to hear only what He would
speak, to see only what He would have it behold,
to touch only at His bidding and to use every
power and capability in and for Him only. It regards itself henceforth as His property, subject to
His disposal and existing for His great purpose regarding it. It is consecrated not so much to the
works, or truth, or the cause, or the church, as to
the Lord. This is done gladly, freely, without fear
or reservation, but as a great privilege and honor
to be permitted thus to belong to so great and
good a Master, and have Him undertake so uncongenial a task as our sanctification and exalta-
tion.

This dedication of our spirits can be made in
the very first moment of consecration and before
we have a single conscious experience or feeling
answering to the dedication we make. As empty
vessels, as bare possibilities with nothing in us yet
but the entire consent of our wills to be all that the
Lord would have us, we yield ourselves to God according to His will.

Once for all

This act of dedication should be made once for
all, and then recognized as done and as including

every subsequent act that we may ever renew as we receive more light in detail respecting His will concerning us. It is possible for us, once for all and not knowing perhaps one-thousandth part of all that it means, to give ourselves to God for all that He understands it to mean, and to know henceforth that we are utterly and eternally the Lord's as certainly as we will know that we are the Lord's after we have been a million years in glory.

Yet, after this one comprehensive act of dedication it is quite proper for us, as new light comes to us and we become conscious of new powers or possibilities we can lay at His feet, to say our glad yes to His claim as often as it is renewed. This is only the working out in detail of the all-inclusive consecration that we made at first.

Beloved, have you thus dedicated yourself and your spirit to God? Will you henceforth dare to reckon yourself all the Lord's, and as each new chamber of your higher nature opens to your consciousness, will you gladly put the key to it in His gracious hand and recognize Him as its Owner and Guest?

The sanctified spirit is a spirit filled with the presence and the Spirit of the Lord. What it gives to Him is only a possibility; His presence alone makes it a reality. Even when dedicated, it is but a vessel, empty and meet for the Master's use. It is He who fills it and pours it out for the supply of the needs of others or to satisfy the desire of His own heart. Even the consecration that we make to God, the very act of dedication itself, has to be made perfect by His grace. We cannot even yield ourselves to Him in a manner that is without imperfection, but we can choose to be His. Then He will come into our dedicated wills and make the living sacrifice worthy of His holy altar.

We can lie down upon that altar in full surrender and because He, the great Burnt-Offering, offered Himself to God for us, once for all, we too can become to God a sacrifice of sweet-smelling savor. This was really the meaning of the Burnt-Offering of old. The offerer did not offer himself, but touched the spotless lamb and it became the perfect offering. So with our hand upon the head of Christ, our consecration is accepted in Him, and He comes into our wills and our spirits, and so unites Himself with us that the sacrifice is acceptable and complete.

Our knowledge of God and fellowship with Him are dependent upon His own grace to be made effectual. We dedicate our spirits to God. Then He reveals Himself to us, opening the eyes of our understanding, showing us the person of Christ, unfolding His truth to our spiritual apprehension, and making us to see light in His own light.

It is wonderful how the untutored mind will often, in a short time by the simple touch of the Holy Spirit, be filled with the most profound and scriptural teaching of God and the plan of salvation through Christ. We once knew a poor girl who was saved from a life of infamy but had little education. In a few days she rose to the most extraordinary acquaintance with the Scriptures and the whole plan of Redemption through the simple anointing of the Holy Spirit. We simply give to Him our spirits that we may know Him; He fills us with His light and revelation.

We cannot create that image

We choose to be transformed to His image, but we cannot create that image by our own morality or struggles after righteousness. We must be created anew in His likeness by His own Spirit, and stamped with His resemblance by His heavenly seal impressed directly upon our hearts from His hand. He thereby becomes to us our holiness, for Christ is made unto us our sanctification; we are made the righteousness of God in Him. We turn from the sin; choose to be holy; God fills our proffered hand with His own spotless righteousness.

Our faith is the filling of His Spirit and the imparting of the faith of God. We choose to trust and He makes that choice good by enabling us to believe and continue in the faith grounded and settled, and so living by the faith of the Son of God. Our love is but a purpose on our part, the power is His; for when we choose to love He multiplies that love within us and imparts to us His own Spirit and nature which is love. All our struggles will not work up one throb of genuine love to God, but He will breathe His own perfect love into any heart that chooses to make Him the one object of affection.

We cannot love our enemies but we can choose

to love them, and God will make us to love them.
Often we have known consecrated characters
placed in circumstances where they were obliged
to come in contact with uncongenial companions
whom they could not love. Choosing, however, at
His bidding to act in the spirit of love, God has so
inbreathed His very heart, that without a struggle
they could adjust themselves to this relationship
and meet the uncongenial associate or enemy with
quietness, tenderness and a holy desire for his
highest good.

God manifested in us

The power to glorify God is nothing more nor
less than simply to let God Himself be manifested
in us and so glorify Himself; then others will see
Him reflected through us.

Sanctification is thus God's own life in the spirit
that is yielded up to Him to be His dwelling place
and the instrument of His power and will. So also
is it true of our spiritual senses of which we have
spoken. They are sanctified when they become
the organs of God's operation; when our spiritual
eyes are opened by His touch; when our spiritual
taste, and touch, and smell are made alive by His
own quickening life within us.

Now, beloved, have you ever learned this wonderful secret of regenerated spirit and God's
Spirit, the Guest and Occupant of that consecrated abode? Let me explain this somewhat lofty
conception by a simple illustration.

Let a common leather case represent the body.

Within it is a silver casket, which stands for the soul. We touch a spring and it opens and discloses an exquisite golden locket, which we shall consider as the symbol of the spirit or higher nature, and within that golden locket is a place all set with precious gems for a single picture.

Is it empty in your spirit, or is it filled with some other face, or is it dedicated to and occupied by your blessed Lord? Is it His shrine and His home and has He accepted it and made it the seat of His glorious abode and throne of His blessed kingdom of righteousness, peace and joy in the Holy Ghost?

Are there some who read these lines who have not yet even learned the meaning of their own spirit and do not know whether it has yet been quickened from the dead and prepared to be the seat of Christ's indwelling? All that they know of life consists in the physical organism, their mental faculties and their human affections. They have a keen, quick, human life, all aglow with emotion and mental activity, but the spirit sadly is so dead and cold that it has not even caught the grasp of these higher thoughts that we have been contemplating.

Must have another nature

If this is you, beloved, there is one world that you have not yet entered, and that is the eternal world to which you are hastening. The life you are living can never introduce you to the sphere of heavenly beings for "flesh and blood cannot inherit the kingdom of God, nor does the perishable inherit the imperishable" (1 Corinthians 15:50). Your physical life will wither like the flowers of summer, your mental endowments will rise to the highest human rank, but will not touch the joy of that celestial realm. You must have another nature before you can enter the kingdom of heaven. "Unless a man is born again, he cannot see the kingdom of God" (John 3:3).

Just suppose for a moment a man is going to a great musical festival in Germany. He enters the great concert hall but he does not know a single word of the language spoken nor has the faintest germ of musical taste. To him the words are meaningless gutturals, and the notes a jargon of confusing noises. He could understand a problem in mathematics or could discourse with them with eloquence in English on questions of politics or philosophy, however, he is out of place; he does not possess the key to their society or enjoyment.

Also let us suppose the greatest intellectual of earth enters the society of heaven. To him their songs and joys would all seem as incomprehensible as the conversation of a cultivated home circle would be to the little dog that sits at their feet or the canary that sings in the window. It belongs to a different race and cannot touch their world.

Such a man would not have one point of contact with these heavenly beings. It would be another world, a world unknown and barren as a wilderness. From its scenes he would be glad to flee to find some congenial fellowship. He cannot reach its range because it is a spiritual race of beings and he has but an intellectual nature. On the other hand, they would have as little in common with him as his range is infinitely below theirs.

We can imagine the porter of heaven's gates asking him what he knows. He tells the gate-keeper about the lore of classical culture, the mythologies of Greece or the monuments of Egypt. The angel smiles with pity and answers, "Why, these splendid memories of which you speak are not worthy of comparison with the world in which we dwell. The grandest temple of Egypt would not make a pedestal for one of the stairs of heaven."

Perhaps he also tells him of astronomy, the distance or magnitude of the stars. "Why," the angel answers, "we have no need of these dim and distant calculations here. There is not one world we have not visited and we could tell you 10,000 times more of its mysteries than you have ever dreamed of. The glories of these cannot be compared with the glory of Him who sits upon the throne, whom you have not eyes to see, or the sweetness of these redemption songs, which you cannot even hear because you have not ears to hear. One thrill of the rapture we feel you cannot ever know because your heart has not been quickened in one heavenly chord. You do not belong here. You live in the lower realm of mind alone, but this is the home of God and those who have received His nature, His Spirit, and are admitted as His children to dwell in His presence and share

His infinite and everlasting joy."

Beloved, this is the high calling that is given to every one of Adam's race who has heard the gospel. You may become a son of God, you may receive a new spirit which can know and enjoy Him, and that spirit can be so sanctified, so cleansed, so enlarged, so filled with Himself, as to be able to reach the highest sublimity of His grace and glory and joy. Will you separate it from all that defiles and dwarfs it? Will you dedicate it to Him to be exalted to its highest possible destiny and will you henceforth receive Him to be its life and purity, its satisfaction, its nature, and its ALL and in ALL?

These four short lines of simple poetry express the depth and height of holiness, namely, as a great need and an infinite supply for that need in God. Beloved, shall they express your emptiness and your divine filling?

In the heart of man—
    A cry;
In the heart of God—
    Supply.

CHAPTER 3

A Sanctified Soul

W e have already seen in the threefold division of our being that the spirit represents the higher and divine element that knows, trusts, loves, resembles and glorifies God. What then is the soul as distinguished from the spirit and the body, and what is meant by a soul wholly sanctified?

The nature and attributes of the soul

It is not necessary for us to descend into all the depths of psychology and attempt to analyze the manifold attributes and faculties of that wondrous consciousness which God has placed within the breast of every human being. It is enough for the present to observe that every one of us is conscious of, at least, the following four great classes of mental endowment—understanding, tastes, affections, passions and appetites.

The understanding is the seat of intelligence. Many and varied are the chambers in this house. Perhaps primary is that which the philosophers have called perception that fixes its attention upon objects and becomes directly cognizant of things and thoughts.

Next might be intelligence—acquiring knowledge, understanding truth and relations, reasoning, thinking and concluding. To this department also belongs memory, a wondrous attribute that recalls the past and stores up forever the impressions and sensations of the mind to be the source of joy or pain.

Imagination follows next. This faculty gives the soul the power of ignoring space, bringing the distant near and peopling the empty void with the creations of an ideal world that seems as real as the material forms around it.

As the correlative of memory, expectation looks out upon the future with the magnifying glass of imagination. It springs forward on the wings of hope, till time and sense are forgotten in the prospect of the bright vista that opens before.

Amid all this, as the helm of character and the driver of the fiery coursers of the soul, sits reason or judgment—the faculty of comparing or concluding, weighing instructions and deciding courses of action. Sometimes it is called common sense; other times, the exercise of judgment.

All these are but a few of the mental qualities of which each of us is conscious, and which constitute the leading attributes of the soul. When we think how much they have to do with every interest of human life, it is not necessary to show how important it is that they should be sanctified so as to be guarded from error and perversion and used for their highest ends—the glory of God, the good of others and our welfare.

The tastes follow next in order. Each of us possesses certain special talents, mental inclinations and adaptations. While one man is a born musician, another has a genius for painting. One may be a natural architect or sculptor, while others are great inventors or travelers, or poets or writers of fiction.

Each of us then has some special bias of mind, and adaptation is usually indicated by inclination. Each of these tastes needs to be sanctified.

Just as in the class of faculties previously enumerated, where the unholy imagination or the false judgment will lead the literary man to be a prurient Ouida or a passionate Byron, so here, a false taste will make a lover of art into a disseminator of vice. The unhallowed love of music can become a channel for Satan's most insidious temptations, and even the love of beauty and refinement, an instigation to self-adornment, fashionable extravagance and the wild carnival of idolatrous worldliness.

Every one of these tastes came to us originally from God, a Lover of the beautiful who has made everything to reflect His own infinite taste and wisdom. Every one of them, however, may become a minister to self and sin and a source of degradation and defilement. Do we not most earnestly desire that all these gifts of heaven, unbalanced and perverted by the Fall, shall be wholly sanctified?

Affections of the heart

Deeper still, in the soul's innermost chamber dwell the affections of the heart. This is the home of love—the mother's love, the bridegroom's love, the love of the child, the brother, the friend—the ties of kindred, deep fellowships of congenial affinity, and common tastes, dispositions, interests and aims.

We spoke in the former chapter of love as one of the exercises of the sanctified spirit. We referred there to the love that the Holy Spirit gives to the heart, a divine love for the Supreme Object and all others related to Him.

We speak now of the human affections instinctive in the soul, which are not wrong in themselves but that need to be sanctified and lifted above self, sin and excess. Along with these affections are the various passions and emotions—pride, acquisitiveness, anger, emulation, mirth, joy, sorrow and many more—all of which are right or wrong according to their measure, their motive and their limitations. It is possible to be angry and sin not, to be proud without vanity, to emulate without envy, to "eagerly desire the greater gifts" (1 Corinthians 12:31) without avarice, and to be ambitious for the highest recompenses without worldliness in spirit or aim.

Yet all these without the grace of God have become like false lights or reefs of rock and ruin to innumerable human souls, whose very brilliancy of natural endowments and success have but aggravated more totally their destruction.

Lower still in the scale of beings are the appetites and propensities that link the mind with the body, and become the handmaids of the physical organs. These we shall speak of more in detail in connection with the sanctification of the body. It is only necessary here to refer to them as qualities of the mind that touch the physical senses and act through them.

All these appetites are natural and, in a properly balanced and sanctified being, are sinless and blameless. The disturbing influences of the Fall and the perversion of human nature, however, have disturbed them from their true order and subordinate place, and have made them become, in many cases, degrading and destructive.

A man whose reasons and affections are under the control of his appetites has started downward on the steep incline which soon must bring him to the level of the brutes, nay, to a still deeper plunge, measured from the height from which he fell. This, at last, is the wretched and hideous condition of many a human soul. It demonstrates the supreme necessity for the appetites and propensities that link us so closely with the brute to be wholly sanctified.

This is a brief survey of the human soul. To realize at once its grandeur and its peril we have only to think of the records of human history. How clear and lofty the intellects that have searched out and sought to teach the ages the principles of truth!

How wonderful the achievements, even without God's light, of Plato, Socrates, Confucius and Seneca! How sublime the genius and imagination of Homer, Virgil, Dante and Shakespeare! How splendid the force of Alexander and Napoleon! How superb the taste of Phidias, Wren, Raphael and Michelangelo! How glowing and glorious the eloquence of Demosthenes, Cicero, Chatham! Yet withal, how sad the highest issues of human culture and wisdom! How bitter and disappointing the brightest prospects to which the best of them could look and how fearful the wreck to which many of them plunged even before the eternal depths were revealed to view! How frequently the brightest intellects have the saddest lives, and how extreme the perils that encompass the path of genius, success or beauty! Oh, how the world needs the Sanctifier to guard even her richest treasures from being their own destroyers!

What is meant by the sanctification of the soul?

How are all these attributes and faculties to be wholly sanctified? Well, we cannot better make this plain than by applying our three simple tests in detail to each of them. They can be separated, dedicated and filled with the Spirit and life of God and thus, in no other way, can they be wholly sanctified. Let's apply the tests in detail.

Is our understanding separated? Have we learned to withdraw our attention and perception from all that is unholy and to refuse to see forbidden things? Is not this the real source of most of our difficulties about a holy life? We allow the unholy world to sweep in through all the avenues of our beings and absorb all our attention until there is inevitable pollution and misery.

The very first thing therefore for us to do is to close the hatches and keep out the billows, to close the shutters and exclude the objects that intrude themselves upon our gaze, to drop the eyelash and be kept as the apple of His eye from the seeing of evil. We can refuse to perceive and notice the evil around us.

As you walk down the street, have you ever been conscious of two forces, the one holding your attention to God in a spirit of quiet recollection and communion, the other tempting you to look at everything on the street—the glare of the shop windows, the busy crowd, the whole animated scene and many a picture of evil—which, if it does not defile, distracts you from the simplicity of your spirit? Have you never felt, on glancing over your morning paper, a check upon your mind as your eye fell upon the glaring columns and a voice that seemed to hold you from absorbing with your eye all the reeking filth that literary scavengers had shoveled from the alleys and garrets of a wicked metropolis? Have you not felt, when you had read it, all saturated with uncleanness, even though you yourself had not any participation in these crimes? Your thoughts had touched them and therefore were defiled?

I was once tempted to read Robert Ingersol's lectures with a view of answering them, but after reading a single page I felt so deluged with the shower of brimstone that poured from every page upon my whole being that I dared not go farther. I felt that I could only warn my people from any contact with such things, and tell them that *evil communications corrupt good manners,* and that God's ground was to abstain from the very appearance of evil and have no fellowship with the unfruitful works of darkness, not even so far as to hear them.

I was once called upon by a young convert, a very earnest Christian woman, who had gone one Sunday night, under strong pressure, to hear this daring blasphemer. Her face was fairly shining with the light of the pit, and she had called to tell me, her pastor, that she was fascinated and knew not what the matter was. She had been so captivated by his brilliant blasphemy that she seemed to have lost her power of resisting.

The very first thing therefore in the sanctification of the mind is to separate it from all evil. Absolutely ignore evil and refuse any contact with it.

Separate ourselves from thoughts

We also should separate ourselves from thoughts as well as objects that are not purifying. There are 10,000 inward activities which spring up in the soul without any touch from the external world or any observation of people or things. Many of these are evil thoughts, and still more of them are unnecessary thoughts. These we must suppress.

It is possible to so hold the reins of the mind

that it will refuse to dwell upon thoughts which the judgment denies. It may be like the waves that beat against the vessel's timbers, but this is very different from letting them into the hold through the hatches. We can keep the hatches down and refuse to open them. If we do so, God will take our thoughts and hold them captive and fill our minds with His higher, holier thoughts.

A great many people wear their minds out with useless thinking. Much of the waste of brain and the dead pain in the cerebellum is not due to over-work for God, but is due to a thousand cares and questions which did nobody any good and did us infinite harm.

A sanctified soul is one that has learned to be still and cease from all its own activities. This is the meaning of the psalmist's passionate cry when wearied with his own exhausting activity, "I hate double-minded men, but I love your law" (Psalm 119:113). This is the meaning of the apostle when he says in Second Corinthians 10:4–5,

> The weapons we fight with are not the weapons of the world. On the contrary, they have divine power to demolish strongholds. We demolish arguments and every preten-sion that sets itself up against the knowledge of God, and we take captive every thought to make it obedient to Christ.

Our imaginations and thoughts must be sup-pressed until we learn to wait in stillness for God's voice and God's thoughts. In that way we will save ourselves needless exhaustion and ever be within touch of God and out of innumerable sources of temptation. For every one of Satan's wandering thoughts is like a thistledown with wings at one end and a seed of evil at the other. Softly it floats into the soul, but everywhere it goes, it deposits its little germ in the fertile soil which brings forth its harvest of poisonous thorns.

We also must cease from the unholy activities of the memory as it dwells on the forbidden past and of the imagination as it builds its vain castles in the air or makes temptation vivid and real before the fascinated soul. We must learn to cease from these activities, to distrust them independently of the Spirit's guidance, and the Master's will, and to hold ourselves unto God for His complete direction and possession.

Are the faculties of the understanding dedicated? Is our attention dedicated to God? Can we say, *My heart is fixed, my mind is stayed on Thee?* Are our thoughts dedicated to God? Is our intelligence devoted to know His Word and will, and to "consider everything a loss compared to the surpassing greatness of knowing Christ Jesus my Lord?" (Philippians 3:8). Is our memory dedicated to be stored with His truth? Does our imagination dwell upon His Word until it makes the things of eternity more real and vivid than the objects of sense? Is our whole power of thought and reason and judgment and decision wholly yielded to Him, to know and do His will?

He is the Author of our intellect, has made it for Himself. It can find its loftiest employment and satisfaction only in God and His Word. He needs our minds as well as our spirits to use as the instruments and organs of His high and holy service.

Understanding and intellect

Is our understanding and intellect filled with God? He must possess us Himself and put in us His thought and mind as well as His spirit and grace. The Christ who came to give Himself to us had not only a divine nature but also a reasonable soul. This He imparts to us in our union with His person. We have the mind of Christ. Into this weak and erring brain can come the very understanding of our blessed Master, so that, as John Kepler, we may say, "I am thinking God's thoughts after God."

The Holy Spirit is a quickening force to the consecrated intellect. Minds that have been dull and obscure before have risen beneath His touch to the highest intellectual attainments and the mightiest achievements of human genius. Every intelligent Christian knows the story of Augustine, the worn-out wreck, who emerged from a wasted youth to become, by the power of grace, the teacher to 12 centuries and the father of evangelical theology.

Another lost intellectual was Thomas Chalmers until kindled from above by the power of grace and a divine enthusiasm. From that hour he became the leader of the religious thought and life of the country and his age.

Such again, in the higher ranks of life, was Wilberforce. As a young, aristocratic Englishman, his early years were frittered away in the frivolities of fashionable life and his mind seemed to have but little force and brilliancy. From the hour in which he gave himself to God, however, every power in his intellect seemed to be awakened and intensified until he became the champion of the greatest movement of modern philanthropy and the honored and successful leader of his country in one of the greatest social movements of English history.

Likewise many a humble name—Harry Moorhouse from the ranks of English pickpockets, Jerry McAuley from the wharf thieves of New York, Dwight Moody from the shoemaker apprentices of Boston—and a great multitude of the most gifted ministers, evangelists and Christian workers of today owe their mental force, and that combination of qualities which constitutes real genius, to the touch of God upon a mind which, without His grace and quickening life, would never have risen above obscurity. The Lord Jesus, being willing to possess the understanding and all faculties and so fill them with His Word and the power of presenting it effectually to others constitutes a new era in the work of God as wonderful as the healing of the body or the consecration of the spirit.

There is a distinct baptism of the Holy Ghost for the mind as well as for the spirit. The latter gives the qualities of earnestness, faith, love, courage, unction and heavenly fire; the former, soundness of judgment, clearness of expression, pungency of thought, power of utterance, attractiveness of style—all those qualities which can fit us to be meet vessels for the Master's use, prepared unto every good work.

A Christian lady recently illustrated this in a simple conversation by telling of a vision that had come to her while praying to God to give her power to understand His Word and teach it to others. She said that there suddenly appeared before her mind, so vividly that it almost seemed real, a naked and empty skull. It almost terrified her at first for it seemed to hint to her some message of death. It was immediately followed, however, by the picture of a flaming fire that seemed to enter the empty skull and fill it in every part. Then a thought was whispered to her heart, "This is the answer to your prayer. Your busy brain must become as dead and empty as that skull and then the Holy Ghost will fill it with His glowing fire and His quickened life; bringing His thoughts and feelings, and taking possession of it as His simple instrument and the organ of His working and His will." This is, perhaps, the most perfect figure by which we can express the thought of this message.

Shall we not, beloved, prostrate our proud intellects and lay our wisdom low at Jesus' feet, and, into brains emptied of their self-consciousness and self-sufficiency, receive the baptism of His fire? Shall we not with a new sense of His meaning breathe out the prayer:

Refining fire go through my heart,
   Illuminate my soul,
Scatter thy life though every part,
   And sanctify the whole.

Separate our tastes

Are the tastes separated? To this point we have spoken only of the understanding and intellect, the thinking, reasoning faculties of the mind, but we have seen that there are other departments. There are the tastes that give direction to our mental faculties, bias to our choice, and zest to our employments.

Love of music

Take, for example, the love of music. It is not necessary to show how it may be and frequently is perverted for worldliness, selfishness and sin. It is the very handmaid of vice and the fascination that allures the heedless world from God and all thought of eternity and salvation.

Yet it is a divine gift and may be wholly sanctified and gloriously used. But it must be separated from all earthly alloy and sinful defilement. The voice that sings for God must not be prostituted to the indulgence of worldliness and sensuality. How often the lips that lead the worship of Jehovah in the sanctuary on Sabbath are found ministering to an ungodly or even to the promiscuous crowd of the music hall or the nightclub before the next six days are ended!

One of Germany's greatest painters refused to

use his brush, when offered a fortune by Napoleon, to paint a Venus for the Louvre. He said that he had just painted the face of Jesus and his art might never be desecrated again.

Well I remember the cloud of condemnation that fell upon my spirit when listening once in my own parlors to the leader of my choir singing the famous "Ave Maria." I could not imagine what had come over my spirit until I began to think of the words and remember that they were words addressed to a human being that belonged only to Jehovah, and I could find no peace until I kindly but firmly bore witness to my dear brother, and promised God that I would never again listen to such blasphemy without faithful protest. Yet how often Christians allow their ears to be defiled by listening to unholy strains by their love of music, and their own voices to be prostituted by unholy performances in the concert or even the private drawing-room.

This taste not only must be separated, but also it must be dedicated to God and used for His service and glory. Then He will fill it with His own anointing and use it to work most gloriously. What ministry today has been more honored than gospel song? How God has shown in a Bliss, Sankey or a Phillips the honor He still will put on this simple taste to draw millions by the power of the consecrated melody of the gospel.

Love of art

The love of art also must be separated. How

many Christian homes there are whose decorations or adornments do not speak for God, but for pagan licentiousness or godless display. This quality of taste may be separated in the matter of personal dress or adorning from that which speaks for the world and self rather than the meek and lowly Jesus. We may dedicate these tastes so that they may be witnesses for Christ. The walls of our chambers shall speak for Him, and our very wardrobe shall be like the phylacteries of Hebrew garments, written over by the sacred characters which declare the glory of our Lord.

Our talents

Then our various talents and the qualities that bring us success in the occupations of life may be separated so that we shall be strong in every direction, not for self or earthly glory, but for our Master's service and our highest usefulness. There is nothing that may speak more for God than refinement, good taste and preeminent talents.

God wants these things inscribed with "Holiness to the Lord" (Exodus 39:40). Blessed be His name for many a lovely woman and many a gifted man who have laid all the attractions of their person and their mind on His altar. May the day be hastened when all that is lovely in the endowments of nature and the gifts of His infinite taste and wisdom shall become garlands for His brow and attributes to lay at His feet to whom belong the beauty and the glory, the riches and the honor, the praise and the love of the whole creation!

Separate emotions and affections

Are the heart's emotions and affections separated? There still remains the most interesting class of our mental qualities, namely, the emotions and affections of the heart. These, we have seen, belong to the human soul.

Above them all is the attribute of love. It is instinctive in some form in every human heart. While there is a divine love which is imparted by the Spirit, the soul is endued by the Creator with a strange and exquisite power of loving. Like the tendrils of a living vine, its cords must reach out in some direction.

How necessary it is that our love should be separated for it is natural for the heart, like the vine, to cling to some rotten and ruined wall, from which it must be detached to save it from destruction. Who is there that has reached the high and heavenly place in the consecrated life who does not look back, in the very beginning of his or her progress, to a lonely grave where the heart's first idols were buried beneath the cross of Jesus, and it died to that which was most dear to every natural instinct and affection?

The path of holiness with us all began at Mount Moriah, in the altar of Isaac, and the sacrifice of our hearts. It is on the same glorious mount that the majestic temple still rises above the spot where the heart in consecration first gave its all to God.

Built on the altar of sacrifice

God loves to build His temples still on the site of the altar of sacrifice. It is not that He takes delight in wrenching our affections, but these objects of love most frequently are draining our heart's very life and must be severed like the succulent growth of a plant, if it is ever to bring forth fruit. Happy are they who, before they unite their hearts to any objects, first learn the mind and will of God and save themselves from a broken heart. It is not necessary that we should be torn from everything we love, if we first learn the mind and will of God.

This is separation. This also is dedication, to give the mind to God and ever to give Him the supreme place in its affections.

Beloved, are you thus separated? Are you willing to separate your heart and your love from all forbidden love, every unhallowed friendship and every purely selfish affection, and to let Christ be the Master of your heart and its chief object of affection and delight? Then He will fill that heart and adjust all its chords to harmony and happiness. Into every relationship of life He will so infuse His own Spirit that we will be enabled to adjust ourselves to all our mingled and manifold situations and relationships so that everyone will be a link with Him and a channel of holy service and blessing.

With these emotions we could trace through the whole realm of our emotional nature and find that there is not one of our affections and even passions which might not have a holy and sanctified use. Our anger may be so pure that it shall be a holy zeal for God. Our emulation may be so free from envy that it shall impel us to imitate the noble qualities of others. Our acquisitiveness may be so regulated that it may be lifted above avarice and covet earnestly only the best gifts. Our ambition may be so heavenly that it shall be an impulse to others, pressing us forward to the most noble achievements and enduring rewards. Every throb of joy and sorrow, hope or fear, may be a movement of the heart of Christ along the various chords of our consecrated being, until every voice within us shall join the heavenly chorus, singing evermore, "To him who sits on the throne and to the Lamb be praise and honor and glory and power, for ever and ever!" (Revelation 5:13).

CHAPTER 4

A Sanctified Body

The human body has been called the microcosm of the universe—a little world of wonders and a monument of divine wisdom and power—sufficient to convince the most incredulous mind of the existence of the Great Designer. There are enough evidences of supreme skill in the structure of the human hand alone to prove the existence, intelligence and benevolence of God in the face of all the sophistry of infidelity.

The records of Creation teach the importance and dignity of the human body. When God had made all other parts of the material universe and before He formed the human frame, He called a solemn council of the Trinity. With the most majestic deliberation He decreed, *Let us make man in our image after our likeness,* and it is added, "And the Lord God formed man from the dust of the ground and breathed into his nostrils the breath of life" (Genesis 2:7). All the infinite wisdom of the

Trinity was concentrated in his creation and the kiss of the Almighty awoke his higher nature into consciousness and life.

The reason God has so honored the human frame is made very clear in the subsequent revelation of Jesus Christ and the great mystery of the Incarnation. The human body was designed to be the ultimate climax of the whole creation and later to be the eternal form of the incarnate God himself. Always, it would seem, that the Lord Jesus Christ had purposed to become embodied in a human form in order to link the creation with the Creator in His own wonderful Person. The human body, therefore, was designed, in the beginning, as the pattern and type of this sublimest form of being which ever should exist.

Have we ever fully realized the stupendous fact that throughout eternity when each new inhabitant shall come to the great metropolis of the universe to gaze upon the face of its Lord, behold the wonderful God to whom all creation owes its existence, and celebrate His yet more wonderful glory and grace in the redemption of a sinful race, He shall gaze upon the face of a man. He shall look upon a form like yours and mine, upon the human frame and countenance of Jesus. Oh! may we still say, *Lord, what is man that Thou has set such honor upon him!*

Our hearts sink in amazement and adoration at the infinite grace which has so glorified the human body. Shall we wonder, therefore, beloved, that God should require it to be made worthy of such a destiny and sanctified wholly unto its high calling! For, seated by the side of that wondrous Man, we, too, shall share His glory, and be the objects of the wonder and love of the ages to come.

A Grave error

One of the gravest errors of all the centuries has been to depreciate the body. Today the old form of gnosticism has been trying to establish the doctrine that matter is not real and that the human body is not real but a fiction. They are pleased to phrase it, "a wrong belief," and state that this "wrong belief" is the cause of all our physical troubles. The aim, therefore, of their long-ago exploded philosophy is to do away with the body, or rather, the belief of the body, and to reduce man to a simple combination of mental faculties. This is wholly contrary to the teachings of Scripture, and would seem to be the antichrist of which the Apostle John declared that it should deny that Jesus Christ had come in the flesh.

Another ancient error was that the body was essentially evil and the great source of temptation and sin, so that the true aim of life in the struggle after sanctity was to get rid of the body, or, at least, to reduce it to the lowest possible condition and render it as incapable as possible of injuring the soul and spirit. One favorite method was the mortification of the body through physical penances and privations until it became reduced and emaciated, so as to cease to be the instigator of evil. The ascetic idea grew out of this delusion.

The essential principle of monasticism is the denying of the body in order to attain the higher culture of the spiritual life.

A still grosser form of delusion taught that the true way to purify the body was to indulge its grossest passions to the utmost excess. This wears it out by its abuse and makes the theory prove its extreme folly in the fact that while professing sanctity it really led to every kind of sin.

The blessed Holy Spirit has taught us a more excellent way. Christ has made provision for the sanctification of the body as well as the soul and spirit. Let us ask once more what is a sanctified body, and the first answer will be:

A separated body

It is essential in order to experience the true sanctification of the body that it be cleansed from all impurity and physical sin. There are bodily transgressions as distinct as those of the soul and spirit.

A sanctified body is a body cleansed from gross, sensual indulgences. This is one of the things of which the Apostle Paul most frequently speaks in those epistles which rise to the sublimest heights of spiritual exultation. It speaks most freely of our high place in the fellowship of Christ and the life of the Spirit. Those who dwell in heavenly places are not exempt from watching diligently against the sins of the flesh.

Beloved, are your bodies thus separated from all unholy use and all abuse?

The sanctified body is a body cleansed from the indulgences of the appetites in every excessive or unnatural form. It is a body that abhors the coarse sin of gluttony and the pampering of its tastes. It is a body that regards the question of eating and drinking, not as a matter for the delectation of the palate, but as a natural and divine provision for its strength and nourishment, that it may glorify God by the use of its powers for Him. It is a body that abstains from the gross and abominable indulgence of the drunkard.

We believe truly, that, in this day, a wholly sanctified body will be kept from even using that which becomes to such multitudes the very poison of hell and the cause of wreck for time and eternity. It is a body that avoids unnatural physical appetites, whether they be the opiate, the cigar or the wine cup.

Beloved, are your bodies thus sanctified and separated from all evil?

The sanctified body is a body whose hands are clean. The stain of dishonesty is not on them. The withering blight of ill-gotten gain has not blistered them. The mark of violence is not found upon them. They have been separated from every occupation that could displease God or injure a fellow man.

A sanctified body is a body whose feet are cleansed from every false way and unhallowed step. They go not in the paths of sinners and the promenades of worldliness and folly. They are not found in the great procession that throngs the theaters and keeps time in the dance to the carnival of folly and earthly pleasure. They walk not in the broad road that leads to destruction, but have turned aside from every forbidden way to walk in the footprints of the Lord, to carry His message and to do His will.

Appearance of the tongue

A sanctified body is a body that is known, as physical health is known, by the appearance of the tongue. Just as a physician asks to see your tongue when he or she examines you, there is no surer test of a sanctified body than the condition of its tongue. A sanctified tongue is a true tongue. It is cleansed from every form of falsehood, equivocation, deception and lying, whether it be the daring perjury of the criminal, or the polite prevarication of fashionable society. Along with this it has also abandoned profanity in every form, the oath of the blasphemer or the polite jest that plays and puns on sacred things and makes light of the holy and the divine. It is a tongue that is free from folly and frivolity. It does not shrink from the spirit of genial and innocent humor when it is controlled by sense and kindness, but it has repudiated foolish talking which is not convenient, and seeks, in everything, to speak in the sight of God as the instrument of His thought and will.

Above all other forms of abuse of the tongue, it has put away evil speaking, the abominable gossip of society, the habit of repeating all that one hears, and especially the evil that affects another. It dare not give publicity to an unkind report or an unfavorable whisper respecting another's character, or even utter that which it knows to be false, unless under the stern necessity of protecting another's soul from danger, and then only when it has first spoken freely and plainly to the offending one directly. A sanctified tongue is also cleansed from all needless speaking. It has learned the golden habit of stillness and finds its greatest blessing in its own suppression and habit of silence and communion with God.

Beloved, has God sanctified your tongue? Are you willing that He should? Will you give to Him the reins of this member, and, henceforth, relinquish to Him the right to hold it in suppression, to keep it from idle, evil, false or foolish speech, and use it wholly as the instrument of His will and service?

Solemnly and forcibly has the Apostle James said: "The tongue also is a fire, a world of evil among the parts of the body. It corrupts the whole person, sets the whole course of his life on fire, and is itself set on fire by hell" (James 3:2).

The sanctified body is a body that has been cleansed from the sins of the eyes. It has purposed that it will not look on evil nor on vanity. It refuses to see the faults of others or to dwell upon the spectacle of temptation or the fascinations of vice. It declines to read double-inked lines that flash, through our daily press, the foul deeds of a fallen world before the eyes of the public, and keeps the spirit pure by closing the shutters of vision and keeping out the foul images that pass before the windows of the heart for all that will allow them to attract their attention. It is a great thing to learn to turn away your eyes from beholding vanity and to remember the injunction of the wisest preacher:

Let your eyes look straight ahead,
    fix your gaze directly before you.
Make level paths for your feet
    and take only ways that are firm.
        (Proverbs 4:25–26)

Beloved, have you sanctified your eyes and separated them from evil unto the Lord, or will you do so from this moment as the light of conviction is passing even now through your soul? Shall you not say,

Take my eyes and let them see
Only that which pleases Thee?

The sanctified body is a body that has cleansed its sense of hearing and put up curtains on its ears against all the sin that assaults our senses from without. It refuses to hear evil as much as to speak it, and puts gossip and slander to flight by looking boldly in its face, and demanding, "How dare you."

Beloved, are you one of those of whom it is written

Who stops his ears against plots of murder
    and shuts his eyes against contemplating
        evil—

this is the man who will dwell on the heights,
　whose refuge will be the mountain fortress
　. . .
Your eyes will see the king in his beauty
　and view a land that stretches afar.
　　(Isaiah 33:15–17)

The sanctified body is a body whose dress is free from worldliness and sin, and marked by that modesty and simplicity that neither attracts attention by its being excessive or defective. The truest dress is that which the ordinary observer is less likely to notice. It is so controlled by simplicity and propriety that most persons should fail to remember anything special in the appearance of the wearer and of which it could be truly said that the wearer was equally unconscious of his or her apparel. There is much in this that speaks for God or the world. Is your dress sanctified to the Lord? Is your person a simple, earnest, modest witness for Christ?

The sanctified body is a body that has been purified from intemperate work, immoderate and excessive service of any kind, and the needless neglect of the simple laws of nature and of health. These efforts should not bind us where God's work or will requires us to go to the extreme of toil and self-sacrifice and self-denial; yet where such denials are needless, they are wrong. It is especially a physical sin for men and women to violate every principle of prudence in the pursuit of pleasure or selfish gain and receive the sad retribution in worn-out bodies and premature disease and death, in pursuit of the fancied prize.

The sanctified body is a body that has been, or at least should be, separated from disease. We do not say that disease is a voluntary sin, but we do say that it is a blemish and a physical impurity. It is a form of corruption in the flesh. Under the ancient dispensation it disqualified priests from ministering at the altar. It was a defilement or blemish, and so still it is a hindrance to the highest spiritual state and to the most effective service for God.

No doubt He can overrule it for much good. He can make the invalid's chamber a beautiful example and testimony. But this does not make the disease the more pleasing to Him nor the less a blemish, an abnormal condition, an impurity in the human system, something from which Christ has come to separate His people, something which He bore upon the cross that we might not bear it, but "by his wounds you have been healed" (1 Peter 2:24).

Beloved, have you been separated from disease, from the malarias and humors that defile your blood, depress your liver, drag down your spirits, cloud your brain, irritate your temper, and overshadow all your future life and work, besides holding you back from service for God, and occupying your existence with a morbid self-consciousness and a struggle that is dragging you down when God wants every power engaged in service for a suffering world? Are you willing to be sanctified from disease? Is it valuable enough for you to throw your prejudices away and accept the salvation that Christ has come to bring for spirit, soul and body?

A *dedicated body*

In the 12th chapter of Romans the Apostle Paul beseeches us to present our bodies a living sacrifice. In a later epistle he speaks to the Corinthians as not their own but bought with a price, therefore expected to glorify God in their bodies which are His. It is impossible for the spirit and soul to be consecrated to God while the body is still held in our own hands, in some measure at least. This is as incongruous as a house presented to a friend while we retain the title deed to the lot on which it stands, or a precious jewel while we retain the key of its casket.

The dedication of the body implies the setting apart of our entire physical beings with every organ and member as the property of God, the object of His special care, and the instrument of His special will and service. While it may be done in one great comprehensive act, once for all, it adds great force and definiteness to it to make it explicit and to recognize every individual member as particularly yielded to His ownership and control. Millions have probably been helped to such a consecration by the eloquent yet simple hymn of Frances Ridley Havergal:

Take my life and let it be
Consecrated, Lord, to Thee;

Take my hands and let them move
At the impulse of Thy love.

We are so prone to generalize things that it is extremely wholesome for us to make our spiritual acts explicit. A consecrated body is one that recognizes itself as the property of God and recognizes Him as the Guardian and Keeper of all its interests and needs. He is responsible to take care of us, and, like little children, we look to Him for all. It is a body that has learned to regard every sense and organ, not as a minister of our own pleasure, but a channel for His life and a weapon for His work.

This, indeed, is the word used by the apostle when he says, "offer yourselves to God, as those who have been brought from death to life; and offer the parts of your body to him as instruments of righteousness" (Romans 6:13). The hands are presented to Him to work for His glory, whether it be in our secular calling or in our ministry for others. This, of course, implies that our works are consecrated as are our greetings. Even the grasp of our hands speaks for Christ.

It means that our tongues speak only at His bidding and for His glory. We regard every word as a trust or service and our speech is always with grace seasoned with salt for the edification of others. A consecrated tongue will not speak even the commonest word without waiting upon God for His direction, and looking to Him for His approval.

Consecrated ears will be very attentive to all that He would have us hear, as well as dead to all other voices. Consecrated eyes will see a thousand opportunities that others pass by unheeded, a thousand beauties and meanings in things that others miss.

Consecrated feet will find the path of duty always easy. The highest stairs, the loneliest walks, the most repulsive journeys, the most self-denying tasks will be a willing service for their Lord. And the errands on which they run will be doubly effectual because they are the Lord's feet which carry the Lord's messages. A consecrated voice will have a new power to sing and speak, which natural tones and cultured elocution or music could never accomplish.

Beloved, are your bodies thus consecrated with all their powers to work and walk and speak, to see and hear, to give of your means and to use your whole external life as a glad and sacred ministry for Christ?

A body filled with the Holy Ghost

"Do you not know that your body is a temple of the Holy Spirit, who is in you, whom you have received from God? You are not your own" (1 Corinthians 6:19). There are many who have received the Master into their hearts whose flesh has not become His entire abode.

None of us yet fully realize to how great an extent our physical frame may become the abode of the Lord Jesus. We have sometimes seen a human face light up with the glory of God in some hour of spiritual elevation, on some mountaintop of spiritual experience, or in the light of the border-land. It seemed as if the body had become trans-parent and the light of heaven within was shining through the windows of a palace.

We are told in the New Testament that Christ has become the Head of the human body, and that even in this life "the body is . . . for the Lord, and the Lord for the body" (1 Corinthians 6:13). He is, it is true, the source of physical strength and health, but there is something far higher than di-vine healing, and that is divine health. It is one thing to have the Lord touch us until we are deliv-ered from our infirmities, but it is another thing to have Him possess us with His life, and our lives become His life manifest in our mortal flesh.

This is the teaching of the apostle in Second Corinthians 4:7: "But we have this treasure in jars of clay to show that this all-surpassing power is from God and not from us" The vessel may be very frail, but if the life of Christ possesses us He fills us with strength as well as divine sacredness. This is what Paul means when he speaks in the verses that follow of being cast down but not de-stroyed, perplexed but not in despair, always bear-ing about in the body the dying of the Lord Jesus, that the life of Jesus also might be made manifest in us.

This life will carry us above our physical infir-mities on the high tide of a supernatural vitality which is not dependent upon our organic conditions. It elevates us above them and becomes a heavenly nourishment to all our conscious life and work, so that we can truly say, "man does not live on bread alone but on every word that comes from the mouth of the Lord" (Deuteronomy 8:3) and that "in him we live and move and have our being" (Acts 17:28).

This is really a foretaste of the future life. The frail vessel of clay cannot bear it all as the resurrection body will be able. We can, however, receive and reflect all that we can hold, in this present mortal life, of the very life of our living, immortal Head, the Second Adam who has been made a quickening Spirit.

Room to receive it

Beloved, have you received this mystery, this new and glorious secret, which all may receive in a cleansed, consecrated and receptive vessel? It is waiting, like the light, to come in wherever there is room to receive it. And this blessed filling not only holds and strengthens, but it endues with power for service, and enables our bodies to become a vehicle of the Spirit and the instrument of the higher nature for the noblest ends.

This great and glorious truth that we have been unfolding is not without a parallel and a parable even in the natural realm. We can often see in the lower world how a piece of clay can be so filled with a higher principle as to be transformed and to be endued with higher properties than its own nature was capable of expressing.

Some examples

Take, for example, that rough mass of iron ore out of the dark mine. It is but a lump of earth, but smelt it, and melt it, cleanse it from all its dross, and draw it out in malleable form into the supple wire that girds, in millions of miles, the whole circle of the globe today. Then fill it with the electric fire, and lo! the earthen vessel becomes the electric wire and speaks the messages of business and affection to all mankind. What a mighty power a piece of clay has become! So God can take your vessel of earth and cleanse, develop, prepare and then fill with His holy presence until it will speak to the millions of earth and the ages of eternity of Him and for Him.

Or, look at two or three chemicals: prepare them, and bring them into chemical adjustments and positions, and then attach suitable wires to form your circle. Let the battery play, and lo! you have the magnificent system of the electric light. Those two little bits of clay suspend between them the most perfect form that science knows today and that is illuminating our streets, our factories, our buildings. So God can take the earthen vessel, and illuminate it with a touch of His glory until it becomes itself the very light of the world.

Or, again, take a little handful of sand and melt it and cast it into your mold. Let it cool, then polish it into a concave lens, and then take it to a splendid observatory and put it into the greatest telescope in the world. Then look into the converging lines of heaven that meet in its bosom, and lo! the whole heavens are revealed, the distant worlds of space have stooped down to meet your eye, and that little bit of clay is filled with the vision of immensity. You can see the distant hills of the moon, the rings of Saturn, the nebulous clouds of space, divided up into their innumerable stars and systems. The whole universe becomes a wonder all through a little bit of clay filled with something higher than itself.

So, beloved, you can be polished and filled until you, too, will shine with the reflected glory of heaven and become a channel for the Spirit of vision and revelation, disclosing the very secrets of the Lord and the wonders of His Word and works.

Or, shall we take another example in that piece of common charcoal? Shall we carry it through all the stages of mineralogy until it becomes crystallized carbon and the rough diamond? Shall we then take it and cut down its rough sides and polish it into facets until from a hundred angles it flashes back the rays of light and the glories of color like a little sun or like a rainbow and sun all combined? It is but a bit of clay filled with light.

So, beloved, these bodies of ours, these earthen vessels, may receive a treasure, too, that will so shine from them, when cleansed and completely sanctified, and when all the Master's discipline has been completed, that it will make them like the sun in the kingdom of their Father.

For the day is coming when the wondering universe will look upon us in the image of our glorious Lord. It will wonder which most to wonder at—the Heavenly Bridegroom or the Heavenly Bride. She received all her glory from her more glorious Head and is all the more wonderful because of her humble origin and because of her dark and sinful past.

Oh, let us yield ourselves unto God. Let us receive Him into every pore and fiber of our beings. Let every chord and every member be a channel for His indwelling and inworking, and our whole spirit, soul and body sanctified wholly and presented blameless unto the coming of our Lord Jesus Christ. Then will these bodies leap into that higher plane and rise to that nobler destiny of which He has given us now the earnest and the foretaste even in this mortal flesh.

CHAPTER 5

Preserved Blameless

I t is one thing for the ship to weigh her anchor
and spread her spotless canvas to the breeze,
and sail away with pennants flying and hearts and
hopes beating high with expectation. It is another
thing to meet the howling tempest and the angry
sea and to enter the distant port. The first experience many—perhaps most of us—have begun, but
what will the issues be? And what promises do we
have for the voyage and the haven? How will all
this seem tomorrow, and tomorrow, and six
months from now, when the practical tests of life
will have proved our theories and measured the
real living power of our principles of life and action?

We have been sanctified wholly: how shall we
be preserved blameless? Thank God, there is the
same provision for both, and to both the closing
promise applies: "The one who calls you is faithful
and he will do it" (1 Thessalonians 5:24). Let us
look at God's provision for His consecrated people

and the conditions on which these promises depend.

The promise of our preservation

We find it in the Old Testament benediction: "The Lord bless you and keep you" (Numbers 6:24). We find it again and again in the psalms and prophets: "The Lord watches over you" (Psalm 121:5); "The Lord will keep you from all harm" (Psalm 121:7); "The Lord will watch over your coming and going both now and forevermore" (Psalm 121:8). Even to poor, vacillating Jacob He swears, "I am with you and will watch over you wherever you go, and I will bring you back to this land. I will not leave you until I have done what I have promised you" (Genesis 28:15). Of His vineyard He declares: "I, the Lord, watch over it; I water it continually. I guard it day and night so that no one may harm it" (Isaiah 27:3). "He will guard the feet of his saints" (1 Samuel 2:9) Hannah sings in her song of triumph. And even in our halting, David declares that "though he stumble, he will not fall, for the Lord upholds him with his hand" (Psalm 37:24).

For those who abide in closer fellowship, Isaiah declares, "You will keep in perfect peace him whose mind is steadfast, because he trusts in you" (Isaiah 26:3). This was also the Savior's prayer before He left the disciples: "Holy Father, protect them by the power of your name—the name you gave me—so that they may be one as we are one" (John 17:11); "My prayer is not that you take them out of the world but that you protect them from the evil one" (John 17:15).

Peter declares that we "through faith are shielded by God's power until the coming of the salvation that is ready to be revealed in the last time" (1 Peter 1:5). Paul tells that "the peace of God, which transcends all understanding, will guard your hearts and your minds in Christ Jesus" (Philippians 4:7). And Jude dedicated his epistle "To those who have been called, who are loved by God the Father and kept by Jesus Christ" (Jude 1:1) and closes with a doxology to Him who is "able to keep you from falling and to present you before his glorious presence without fault and with great joy" (Jude 1:24). The Apostle Paul opens his last epistle with the triumphant confession: "I know whom I have believed, and am convinced that he is able to guard what I have entrusted to him for that day" (2 Timothy 1:12), and closes with the yet bolder declaration, and "The Lord will rescue me from every evil attack and will bring me safely to his heavenly kingdom" (2 Timothy 4:18). Such, then, are some of the promises of God's preserving grace.

The provision made for our preservation

It is made in the atonement of Christ. "Because by one sacrifice he has made perfect forever those who are being made holy" (Hebrews 10:14). The death of Christ has purchased our complete and final salvation if we are wholly yielded to Him and do not willfully take ourselves out of His hands and renounce His grace and faithfulness.

It is continued by the intercession of Christ. "Therefore he is able to save completely [or, as it is in the margin, forever] those who come to God through him, because he always lives to intercede for them" (Hebrews 7:25). It is because He always lives to intercede that they are kept; because He lives we shall live also.

This is Paul's meaning when he declares that "For if, when we were God's enemies, we were reconciled to him through the death of his Son, how much more, having been reconciled, shall we be saved through his life!" (Romans 5:10). And so, in Romans 8, he declares: "Christ Jesus, who died—more than that, who was raised to life—is at the right hand of God and is also interceding for us" (verse 34). And then comes the shout, "Who shall separate us from the love of Christ?" (Romans 8:35).

The blood of Christ secures our preservation. For John declares, "if we walk in the light, as he is in the light, we have fellowship with one another, and the blood of Jesus, his Son, purifies us from every sin" (1 John 1:7).

The old ordinance of the red heifer, in Numbers 19, is a beautiful type of Christ's cleansing power. The ashes were preserved and mixed with water, and used as a water of separation, sprinkled upon the unclean, and separating from defilement which had been contracted after the cleansing. It did not refer to the original cleansing, but to the taint that came from the touch of the dead.

We, though wholly separated from evil and dedicated to God, constantly come into contact with evil, and incur defilement from the elements that surround us on every hand. We need constantly, like the washing of the disciples' feet or the bathing every morning of the flower cup in the crystal dewdrop, a fresh application of His blood.

If you ask what this blood means, the answer, perhaps, is a double one. It is the fresh application of His atoning sacrifice by faith and it is an appropriation of His life to our beings, *for the blood is the life.* The blood of Jesus is His risen and divine life imparted to us by the inbreathing of the Holy Spirit and the absorbing power of a living faith. His pure life filling us expels all evil, and continually renews and refreshes our entire being, keeping us ever clean and pure, even as the fresh oil in the lamp maintains the flame, or as the running stream washes and keeps the pebble that lies at the sandy bottom pure.

The abiding presence of Christ and the indwelling of the Holy Spirit are God's chief sources of preservation for His trusting people. It is He who keeps and He keeps from within. "And I will put my Spirit in you and move you to follow my decrees and be careful to keep my laws" (Ezekiel 36:27); "If a man remains in me and I in him, he will bear much fruit" (John 15:5); "No one who lives in him keeps on sinning" (1 John 3:6); "The Lord watches over you" (Psalm 121:5); "The Lord will keep you from all harm" (Psalm 121:7). Another verse that clearly talks of this abiding presence is First John 3:9: "No one who is born of God will continue to sin, because God's seed remains in him; he cannot go on sinning, because he has been born of God." The presence of Jesus comes between us and every temptation, and meets the adversary with vigilant discernment, rejection and victory.

Conditions on which God's keeping depends

All God's promises are linked with certain attitudes on our part. It is the willing mind and the surrendered heart that are assured of God's protection and grace. "God opposes the proud but gives grace to the humble" (James 4:6). "No one who lives in him keeps on sinning" (1 John 3:6). That which is *committed* to Him He is able to keep.

The principle of spiritual perseverance has never been better stated than in Samuel's language to Saul 3,000 years ago: "If you fear the Lord and serve and obey him and do not rebel against his commands, and if both you and the king who reigns over you follow the Lord your God—good" (1 Samuel 12:14).

More particularly is that true if we would be preserved blameless.

Let us expect to be preserved. If we go out anticipating failure we will have it. At the least, we shall never know certainly but that the next temptation we meet is the one in which we are to fall. As the chain is never stronger than its weakest link, we will be sure to fall.

It is the prestige of an army that secures its victory. It is the quickening assurance that it has never been defeated that carries it irresistibly against the foe.

Let us also expect to be tempted. Most persons, after a step of faith, are looking for sunny skies and unruffled seas. When they meet a storm and tempest they are filled with astonishment and perplexity. But this is just what we must expect to meet if we have received anything of the Lord.

The best token of His presence is the adversary's defiance, and the more real our blessing, the more certainly will it be challenged. It is a good thing to go out looking for the worst, and if it comes we are not surprised. But if our path is smooth and our way is unopposed, it is all the more delightful, because it comes as a glad surprise.

Let us, however, completely understand what we mean by temptation. You, especially, who have stepped out with the assurance that you have died to self and sin, may be greatly amazed to find yourself assailed with a tempest of thoughts and feelings that seem to come wholly from within. These will cause you to say, "Why, I thought I was dead, but I seem to be alive."

This, beloved, is the time to remember that temptation has power to penetrate our inmost being with thoughts and feelings that seem to be our own, but are really the instigations of the evil one. *We wrestle with principalities and powers.* That is to say, they twine themselves around us as wrestlers do about the limbs of their opponents, until they seem to be a part of ourselves. This is the essence of temptation. We are almost constrained to conclude that the evil is within ourselves, and that we are not cleansed and sanctified as we had believed. Do not wonder if you are assailed with temptation that comes to you in the most subtle forms, the most insinuating feelings, the most plausible insinuations, and apparently through your inmost being and nature.

Temptation alone is not sin

Temptation is not sin unless it be accompanied with the consent of your will. There may seem to be even the inclination, and yet the real choice of your spirit is fixed immovably against it. God regards it simply as a solicitation, and credits you with an obedience all the more pleasing to Him because the temptation was so strong.

We little know how evil can find access to a pure nature. It seems to incorporate itself with our thoughts and feelings, while at the same time we resist and overcome it. We remain as pure as the sea fowl that emerges from the water without a single drop remaining upon its burnished wing, or as the harp string, which may be struck by a rude and clumsy hand and gives forth a discordant sound, not from any defect of the harp, but because of the hand that touches it. But let the master's hand play upon it and it is a fountain of melody and a chord of exquisite delight.

The truth is that these inner thoughts and suggestions of evil do not spring from our own spirits at all if truly sanctified, but are the voices of the tempter. We must learn to discriminate between his suggestions and our choices, and declare: "I do not accept! I do not consent! I am not responsible! I will not sin! I reckon myself still dead indeed unto sin and alive unto God through Jesus Christ."

There is a most beautiful incident related in the annals of the early Church by Mrs. Jamieson. A holy and exceedingly beautiful maiden in Antioch become the object of the sinful passion of a heathen nobleman. Unable to win her affection, he employed a magician to throw over her a fatal spell and win her in the toils of his snare. The magician himself became enamored of the fair girl, and sold himself to the devil on condition that he should be given power to captivate her with unholy passion. He began to apply all his arts, and throw over her mind the fascinating spell of his own imaginations. Suddenly the poor girl found herself, like a charmed bird, possessed by feelings and apparently by passions to which she had always been a stranger. Her pure heart was horrified by constant visions from which her whole being recoiled, and yet it seemed to her that she must herself be polluted and degraded. She began to lose all hope and to stand on the verge of a despair which was impelling her to throw herself away in hopeless abandonment to the power that possessed her.

In this condition of mind she went to see her bishop. This good man, with quick discernment, immediately pointed out to her that these influences and feelings were not from her own heart at all, but spells from the will of another. Their only power consisted in her fears and her recognition of them as her own. If she would stand firm in her will, refusing in the name of the Lord to acknowledge them as her thoughts, and disdaining either to fear them or for a moment to consent to them, their power would be wholly broken.

Unutterably comforted by this wise counsel, she returned to her home and set her face, in the strength of Christ, against these allurements of evil, and immediately she found them broken. Soon the magician became conscious that his power was ended and came to her in deep contrition, confessing his sin and asking her forgiveness and her prayers. It is said that afterwards he yielded himself to the Lord, having been convicted by the triumph of the grace of Christ through a pure and trusting will.

This little incident tells the whole story. Let us never reckon any temptation to be our own sin, but stand steadfast in our purpose, and God will give us the victory.

Reckon ourselves dead.

Let us continually reckon ourselves to be dead indeed unto sin. We should detach our spirits from every evil thing that touches them, tell the devil that these are his children, not ours. Those temptations he lays at our doors, refuse to acknowledge any relationship with them. Keep the hatches down when the billows sweep the deck, and as long as they do not get into the hold of our little vessel we can sail on not fearing the worst. As we so reckon, Christ will reckon, and make the reckoning true for us.

Let us reckon Christ to be in us and recognize Him as the indwelling Life and Keeper of our spirit, soul and body. It is a great principle that where we recognize God, there God will meet us. Recognize Him in the heavens and He will meet us in the heavens. Recognize Him by our side and He will speak to us from beside us. Recognize Him in our inmost heart and He will meet us there. Let us trust Him as a faithful Keeper. Let us set the Lord always before us, and say with the psalmist: "Because he is at my right hand, I will not be shaken" (Psalm 16:8).

Let us abide in the love of Christ. Let us persuade ourselves that He loves us infinitely and perfectly, delights in us continually, and is wholly committed to us to carry us through and fulfill in us all the good pleasure of His will. Let us not think that we must wring from Him, by hard constraint and persuasion, the blessings which our faith compels. Rather He has set His heart on our highest good and is working out for us, in His loving purpose, all that we can receive of blessing.

Lying like John in His bosom, let us each reckon ourselves to be the disciple whom Jesus loved. Like Enoch, let us claim by faith the testimony that we please God, and looking up with confidence we shall find His responsive smile and benediction. The true secret of pleasing God is to trust Him, believe in His love to us, be artless children and count ourselves beloved of God.

Reasonable and gentle standard

Let us remember that God's will for us is not a hard and impossible task but a reasonable, practicable and gentle standard. He is not continually frowning upon us because we cannot reach some astonishing height, or imitate some prodigy of martyrdom and service, but He expects of us a simple, faithful life in the quiet sphere which He has assigned to us. We are truly blameless in His sight when we are following, moment by moment, His perfect will in life's duties as they meet us.

He adapts the standard of duty according to our circumstances and ability. The parent expects less of the lisping child than the teacher does of the older student or the employer does of the full-grown man. God knows our strength and capacity; His will is adapted to our growth, and His "yoke is easy and [His] burden is light" (Matthew 11:30). Therefore, let us not reprove ourselves because we have not yet reached some ideal that, by and by, we shall have attained to. Are we meeting His will today and saying yes to His claims as the moments pass? Then, indeed, we are blameless in His sight.

At the same time, let us not allow this comfort to allure us to a false extreme. If, on the other hand, God is pressing us forward by His Spirit to higher reaches, let us not be content with less, for we shall not be blameless unless we press forward that we may apprehend all for which we are apprehended of Christ Jesus. With many of us, God is not finding fault for actual disobedience, perhaps, but for shortcoming and a too easy contentment with past attainments. The great question is: Are we obedient to the voice of His Spirit as He calls us onward, step by step?

Implicit obedience

Implicit obedience to every voice of God and every conviction of duty is essential to a blameless life. One moment's hesitation to obey, one act of willful disobedience, will plunge us into darkness, cause withdrawal of His conscious presence from the heart, and leave the soul disarmed and exposed to temptation and sin. Those who have become wholly sanctified have given up the right of self-will and disobedience forever. It is not to be thought of even for a moment that we should hesitate to say yes to His every voice. True, we may not know His voice at all times, but in such cases He will always give us time. When we are convicted of His will and convinced of His way for us, there is no alternative but obedience or a fearful fall and a complete loss of the divine communion.

We must preserve ceaseless communion with God, and abide in the spirit of prayer and fellowship through the Holy Spirit. The interruption of our communion for an hour might lose a step. That lost step might lead us from the pathway of His perfect will and the fellowship of His presence for days to come, or, at least, leave us a step behind, and therefore not blameless.

We must maintain a quiet spirit. It should be free from the turmoil and agitation of anxious care and inward strife, and still enough to always hear His voice. "And the peace of God, which transcends all understanding, will guard your hearts and your minds in Christ Jesus" (Philippians 4:7). This is the soul's defense if we would be preserved blameless. Therefore let the peace of God rule in your hearts, and regard with apprehension and alarm even a moment's interruption of your quietness and inward rest.

We must jealously guard our hearts and thoughts. We should not feel ourselves at liberty to drift into the current of all the imaginations that are ever ready to sweep through the brain, and the idle words in which even Christian people are always ready to involve us. If you are walking closely with God and watching for His voice, you will be quickly conscious of a constraint, a weight upon your mind, a repression upon your heart, a deep tender sense of God's anxiety for His child—the mother calling her little birdlings to her soft wing from the place of peril. Truly "He that guards his lips guards his soul" (Proverbs 13:3). These outward gates are places of danger, and the path of safety is a hidden one.

Live by the moment

We must not live by long intervals, but by the breath

and by the moment. Each instant must be dedicated and presented to God, a ceaseless sacrifice, and each breath be poured into His bosom and received back from His being.

We must learn to recover instantly from failure by frank confession and prompt faith and recommittal. It is possible to catch ourselves before we have really fallen. God does not count it a fall if we do not yield to it. Unseen hands are ever near to bear us up even when we dash our foot against a stone. The remedy is found even before the danger has become effectual.

There is provision for every failure in the blessed promise, "If we confess our sins, he is faithful and just and will forgive us our sins and purify us from all unrighteousness" (1 John 1:9). There is something higher and better than this, the grace that is able to keep us from stumbling, and check us even before the fall is accomplished. So He is willing to keep us even as the apple of the eye, reminded of the danger before it has become fatal, and instinctively closing the eyelids against its intrusion.

Let us remember that the whole spirit, soul and body must be trained to abide in Christ. The life He gives us is not a self-contained endowment but a link of dependence, and every part of our beings must continually draw its replenishment and nurture from our living Head, and thus be preserved blameless unto the coming of our Lord Jesus Christ.

CHAPTER 6

Even as He

J ohn, the apostle of love, gives us a picture of
perfect love, and its source in perfect faith and
union with the Lord Jesus Christ. For this is
the force of the passage: "Love is made complete
among us so that we will have confidence on the
day of judgment, because in this world we are like
him" (1 John 4:17). It is the full realization of our
oneness with Jesus that gives us perfect love.

We are sitting at the feet of the greatest teacher
of love. We are learning from him who himself
leaned on the Master's breast, and learned all he
knew of love from the living touch of His heart.

Perfect love

It is evident that the love he refers to is our love
to God. The phrase, "Perfect love drives out all
fear" (1 John 4:18), explains what he means by
perfect love. It is a love that has no doubt or dread
in it, but leans confidently on the bosom of the
Lord, trusts in the darkest hours with unfaltering

confidence. Even in the day of judgment it will stand with boldness amid the tumult and the wreck of a dissolving world, and claim its place in the friendship of the Judge who sits upon the throne.

During the French War of 1870, a train was carrying military dispatches from Metz to the headquarters of the French army. The Germans had just captured Metz, and were marching rapidly to cut off the French army. It was necessary that the dispatches should reach the post within an hour. The distance was 60 or 70 miles. The road was rough; the train consisted of a single coach and locomotive. The speed was like a whirlwind, and the passengers, consisting of the wife and child of the engineer, the bearer of the dispatches and a newspaper correspondent, were hurled around in the dashing, rushing train, like sailors in a frightful storm.

To say that they were alarmed would be little, for they were in imminent and deadly peril. Every moment threatened to pitch the furious train over some embankment or bridge. Rolling from side to side, leaping at times in the air, rushing, roaring on past stations, everything made way for this whirlwind of desperate speed and energy. The few people inside held their breath in dismay, and often cried out with terror as they dashed along. But there was one person on that car, the little child of the engineer, who knew nothing of their fears. Happy as a bird amid all the excitement around her, she laughed aloud in childish glee and merriment as often as the train would give some wild lurch and hurl her over a seat. When they looked at her in wonder, and her mother asked her if she was not afraid, she looked up and answered: "Why, my father is at the engine!"

A little later the engineer came through the car to cheer up his trembling wife. As he entered with great drops of sweat rolling down his soot-stained face, the little child leaped into his arms and laid her head upon his bosom, as happy and peaceful as if she was lying on her little bed at home. What a picture of the perfect love that casts out fear! What a lesson for the children of the Heavenly Father!

Look at your little, lisping babe putting his hand in yours and letting you lead him where you will, and learn to trust and love the Father who cannot err, forget or fail. This is the remedy for every fear—the fear of man, the fear of yourself, the fear of Satan, the fear of death, the fear of falling, the fear of the future. Only love Him and rest in His love, and you will dwell safely and be quiet from the fear of evil.

What a life ours would be if we were fully saved from our fears! How many of our worst troubles are those that never come! God give us the perfect love that casts out fear!

The secret of this love

"Because in this world we are like him" (1 John 4:17). This love is the fruit of faith. It is the blossom that grows on the fair tree of trust. Its roots are in the very heart of Jesus. Its life is nourished by His very life and love. It is as we realize what He is to us and what we are to Him, that we enter into the fullness of His love.

There is no stronger statement anywhere in God's Word of our intimate and absolute union with the person of the Lord Jesus Christ. It does not mean that some day we shall be like Him, but here, and now, as He is, *so are we in this world.*

We are one with Him in His death. His death was our death,

> For Christ's love compels us, because we are convinced that one died for all, and therefore all died. (2 Corinthians 5:14)

He hung upon the cross in our name, and His dying has as effectually settled all the claims of God's law against us as if we had been executed for our own crimes and had already passed through all the pains and penalties of hell. How can we help loving such a Friend? What will we fear when He Himself has taken our very sins? It is only as we realize this fully that we will live in the perfect love that casts out all fear.

As He is in His Resurrection, so are we in this world. For we are not only dead with Him, but we also live with Him. The life we now live is not the same as our past. The saved man is no longer himself. He is dead, and the man who lives in his stead is a new man in Christ Jesus. He can truly say: "I no longer live, but Christ lives in me" (Galatians 2:20a). It is not the same man. Your old sins are regarded as the sins of another. You are even as He. God recognizes not the old man, but the Christ in you, and receives you as He does His own beloved Son. Why then should you be afraid? Only realize your unity with Him, and His perfect love will cast out all fear.

As He is in his acceptance by the Father, so are we also in this world. For, "he has freely given us [His glorious grace] in the One he loves" (Ephesians 1:6), or, literally, in the Son of His love. That is to say, we are accepted even as the Son of His love is. We are as dear as the Son of His love is. The word *accepted* means received with complacency and delight—God is pleased with us for Jesus' sake, even as He is with Christ Himself.

A Scottish shepherd had a ewe that had lost her lamb, while another lamb was motherless. Vainly he tried to make the lambless mother accept the motherless lamb. She would have nothing to do with it, but pushed it rudely from her with cruel and heartbroken anger, because it only reminded her of the one she had lost.

At length a sudden solution occurred to him. He took the skin of the dead lamb and with it he covered the living one, Then he brought it to the offended mother. Instantly her whole manner changed to the tenderest affection. She welcomed the lamb with a mother's tenderness, caressed it, washed it, fed it from her bosom and treated it as if it were the very lamb she had lost.

So He has made us accepted in the Beloved. So He receives us even as His own dear Son.

We are one with Him

In His ascension glory we are one with Him. His ascension was not for Himself. He has sat down at the right hand of God, far above all principality and power, and every name that is named, not for Himself, but for us. He is there as our Head, we are here as His body. He has taken His seat there in our names, and written our names on the places prepared for us.

Just as you have sometimes gone into some great assembly and held not only your own seat, but also the seats which you have reserved for your friends until they should come, so Jesus is sitting for us on high and holding our places until we go. "He is the head of the body, the church" (Colossians 1:18); "which is his body, the fullness of him who fills everything in every way" (Ephesians 1:23). God always thinks of us as if we were there. Let us think of ourselves and live as in heavenly places in Christ Jesus.

In His redemption, Christ has purchased for us certain rights. To us they are the free gifts of God's mercy, utterly undeserved by us. To Him they are simply the fulfillment of a covenant whose condition He has met, and whose promises He is entitled to claim to the full.

These rights we share with Him. While in one sense, we ourselves have no rights as sinners to anything but punishment and banishment, in union with Him we are entitled to all that He has purchased by His righteousness and blood. We may come to God and claim from His justice and faithfulness all the worth of our Savior's atonement.

Suppose that one of my friends was to go to a leading business house and order for me a large and valuable bill of goods. Then he would send me word that the goods were paid for and that I was requested to go and select the full amount of the deposit.

There would be no modesty in my hesitating to take the very best quality of goods. There would be no kindness to my friend in acting before the clerks of that store as if I was a pauper and receiving a gratuity. My most becoming course would be to act with manly independence and claim the full measure of my friend's purchase.

From my friend it may have been a gift, but for the business house it is a purchase, and fully paid and involving on my part every right of simple justice.

Exactly so, Christ has purchased for us a complete salvation, and paid for it to the full. In His name, we may come and buy *wine and milk*, the choicest blessings, *without money and without price*. We buy without money, because He has paid the price. Yet we buy in the sense of making it absolutely our own.

When we fully realize that we do this by fully standing with Christ in all His rights, we enter into the perfect love that casts out fear. No longer do we hold back, like the prodigal, in the servant's place. Prodigals, indeed, we are, but we have become, in our Elder Brother, more than sons. Let us draw near, therefore, in full assurance and with fearless confidence, and dwell in the Father's house in perfect love.

Children of God

In His Sonship, we become children of God. "I am returning to my Father and your Father, to my God and your God" (John 20:17). Our heavenly sonship is not natural. We are not children of God by virtue of creation, as angels are and Adam was, but through the new birth, initially, which makes us partakers of the divine nature, and, still more, through our personal union with the Lord Jesus Christ, who so comes into us and dwells in us that we partake of His own relation to the Father, and are the children of God, even as He is. This is especially true after we enter into the deeper life of abiding in Christ, and receive the full baptism of the Holy Ghost.

There are two terms used for children in the New Testament. One, *teknon,* meaning a child; the other, *huios,* meaning a son in the most exclusive sense in which the term can be used. Jesus is never called *teknon,* but always *huios—never a child of God, but always the Son of God;* that is, the only begotten and well-beloved Son.

Now, we are called *tekna,* in the Scriptures; that is, the children of God. After a certain point in our experience, the careful student of the original

Scriptures will not fail to notice that the higher word for sonship—the word that exclusively belongs to Jesus—is also given to those who have received Jesus to abide in them. United to Him, they have come into His own very place with the Father, and are the sons of God in the very same sense that He is. Wonderful, glorious place!—that as He is, so are we also!

Even as the wife is received in the husband's home, we are wedded to Him and inherit His high prerogative.

In His Father's love, we are dear to God. There is one thing which the human heart is unwilling to give away to any other and that is the exclusive love which belongs to us alone, from those that are dear to us. We cannot give it away to any unless they are so close to us that they are even as we ourselves. This is the most wonderful thing about the love of Christ. He has given away to His disciples His Father's peculiar love to Him. "That the love you have for me may be in them and that I myself may be in them" (John 17:26).

How can He give to us that sacred love which was His own supreme delight? Only because we are one with Him. In giving it to us, He is only giving it to Himself in another form. It is like the mother willing to share the love of her husband with her child who is part of her own self.

It is the strongest proof of our identity with Christ. For in no other way could He share with us that which belongs to Himself alone. In the same way, we as His disciples, can be willing that

His peculiar love to us should be shared with our brethren, because they are one with us.

Well may it give boldness to our love to know that we are as dear to the Father as His beloved Son, so that Christ must perish before we can be plucked out of His hand.

We are sanctified

In His righteousness and holiness, we are sanctified. "Both the one who makes men holy and those who are made holy are of the same family. So Jesus is not ashamed to call them brothers" (Hebrews 2:11). Our sanctification is the very same as His. He said in His parting prayer, "For them I sanctify myself, that they too may be truly sanctified" (John 17:19).

Christ gives us His own holiness, being made unto us of God sanctification and redemption, and as He is so are we also. This should give boldness to our love. He does not expect of us any qualities that He is not willing Himself to impart. He does not chide us for our failures and imperfections, but because we do not receive more of Him.

Let us, therefore, nestle closer to His breast and throw ourselves more fully upon His all-sufficient grace.

In His mind, we are sufficient for we have the mind of Christ. Humanity is threefold: spirit, soul and body. Christ gives us His soul and life as well as His spirit.

He thinks His thoughts in us and not only reveals to us divine truths, but also gives us a divine capacity to understand them. It is not a similar mind but the same mind that was in Jesus that we are exhorted to possess. How it quickens the languid thought, clarifies the obscure conception, enlarges the vision of the soul, kindles the imagination and inspires every lofty and heavenly impulse to enthusiasm, until the soul takes wings and mounts up into the heights that are to others inaccessible and which are full of glory!

There is no direction in which the life of Christ may be more practical and helpful in our work for Him, than in this connection. Happy are they who have learned to say with the great apostle,

> Not that we are competent to claim anything for ourselves, but our competence comes from God. He has made us competent as ministers of a new covenant—not of the letter but of the Spirit; for the letter kills, but the Spirit gives life. (2 Corinthians 3:5–6)

Friends and colleagues

In His plans and thoughts, we are friends and colleagues. The Master has said as the tenderest expression of His love:

> I no longer call you servants, because a servant does not know his master's business. Instead, I have called you friends, for everything that I learned from my Father I have made known to you. (John 15:15)

We are not working as slaves at a task, but as partners in a blessed fellowship in which we share all the plans and thoughts of our Lord respecting His work. We are not required to go in blind obedience and do simply what we are told, but we are entrusted with His resources and guided by His wisdom. He has unfolded to us the mystery of His kingdom and the great purpose of His providence respecting Israel, the Church and His Second Coming.

We are trusted and confidential friends and fellow workers, and counted true yokefellows with Him in all His cherished thoughts and purposes. Let this inspire us to more loyal service, and fill us with a love that casts out all fear, to know that in all that is dearest to His heart we share His fullest confidence, and as He is so we are in this world.

We have God's fullness

In the indwelling of the Holy Spirit, we have God's fullness. He has given us the very same Spirit that dwelt in Him. On the banks of the Jordan, He first received the Holy Spirit, and as He was leaving the world He breathed upon them and communicated to them with the sweetness of His own life and love the same Spirit in which He had wrought all His miracles and spoken all His words. Peter says in connection with the gift of Pentecost that Christ *"has received from the Father the promised Holy Spirit and has poured out what you now see and hear"* (Acts 2:33b). *The Holy Spirit is called the Spirit of Christ and sometimes even Christ, be-*

cause He brings to us the presence of Jesus and enables us to realize our oneness with Him.

The secret of the love that casts out fear is being filled with the Spirit of Jesus until we are lost in the consciousness of our union with our beloved Lord. "To him God gives the Spirit without limit" (John 3:34). If we have Him we have the Spirit that dwelt in Him without measure.

Have we? Then, indeed, we are *filled with all the fullness of God* and have received " . . . immeasurably more than all we ask or imagine, according to his power that is at work within us" (Ephesians 3:20).

In His physical life we know health. "For we are members of his body" (Ephesians 5:30) and "his life [is] revealed in our mortal body" (2 Corinthians 4:11). This is the secret of divine healing, to be so united with Christ in our body that we will share in these vessels of clay the life and strength of our risen Head.

Even in our physical frames we may be in this world as He is also. This was the secret of Paul's endurance. He could be buffeted by every blast, exposed to every hardship, yet not crushed by any pressure. Sorrowful yet always rejoicing, cast down but not destroyed, shouting mid all the extremes of life's vicissitudes. "I can do everything through him who gives me strength" (Philippians 4:13).

How this experience deepens our love as we look back and remember how often He has relieved our physical sufferings! How many aches and infirmities He has healed or hindered and how tenderly He has cherished our mortal frames, even as a mother does the babe she loves! How our heart swells with the love that casts out fear! How sweet it is to lean our whole weight on Him, knowing that as He is so are we also in this world.

We are remembered

In His ministry of prayer, we are remembered. There is no place where Christ more fully identifies Himself with us than at the mercy seat, where He bids us pray in His name. This means in His very personality, taking the very same place as He Himself and asking all that He is entitled to claim.

Also, He gives us His own Spirit to pray in us, impresses us with His own desires and wishes, and so enables us to pray that it shall be His own very prayer. This is the secret of all true prayer, to pray in the Lord Jesus, asking what He would ask and as He would ask it.

To such prayer the promise is absolute.

My Father will give you whatever you ask in my name. (John 16:23)

If you remain in me and my words remain in you, ask whatever you wish, and it will be given you. (John 15:7)

Therefore, since we have a great high priest who has gone through the heavens, Jesus the Son of God, let us hold firmly to the faith we profess. (Hebrews 4:14)

Let us then approach the throne of grace with confidence, so that we may receive mercy and find grace to help us in our time of need. (4:16)

In our service for Christ, we are in partnership with God. "As you sent me into the world, I have sent them into the world" (John 17:18) is His commission. We are sent into the world as directly as the Lord Jesus Himself was. This was not His home, but He came into it to do a special work for the Father and the world, lived in it as a stranger, and left it when His work was done.

True service for God is not only to do our work as Christ did it, but to do it in the very life and strength of Christ. This is the meaning of the promise, "anyone who has faith in me will do what I have been doing" (John 14:12), that is, He will work in partnership with me, we doing the same works together. This is the same thought as Paul expresses in Ephesians. "For we are God's workmanship, created in Christ Jesus to do good works, which God prepared in advance for us to do" (2:10). Our very works are prepared for us, and inspired in us by the indwelling Christ.

How it fills the heart with love and dispels our fear to know that in all our service for Him, He is with us and in us, and as He is so are we also in this world in all our work for Him.

He suffers in our suffering

In our sufferings, He suffers too. Not only does He

suffer with us in all our trials, but we are called to suffer with Him and to "fill up in my flesh what is still lacking in regard to Christ's afflictions, for the sake of his body, which is the church" (Colossians 1:24). How keenly we often feel the condition of others for whom we are called to pray or to minister! It is only the heart of Christ suffering in us for those whom He would let us help, by bearing their burdens or holding them up for His blessing.

By the sufferings of Christ we do not mean sickness or calamity, but those sufferings that involve the sufferings of others, or sympathy with Him in some place where we can share His burdens. How touching His words to Paul when he was persecuting the saints, "why do you persecute me?" (Acts 26:14). This was the highest ministry of Jesus—to suffer. This is also the crowning ministry of almost every Christian life.

The last two Beatitudes are wholly about suffering, implying surely not only the climax, but a double climax. The dear Scotch martyr, dying at the stake in the Solway Sands, expressed it finely when looking at the little maiden who was dying near her and struggling with the waves in the last conflict, she said, "What do I see but Christ in one of His members suffering there?" It was not Margaret Wilson but Christ suffering there. And so, beloved, you never suffer alone if you suffer for Him and according to His will.

In our faith, we will face trials as He did. Even the power to believe is the working of Christ within us. He is the author and finisher of our faith, and

He will enable us to believe even as He. Christ is the great example of faith; He is its inspiration too.

How sublime the faith that trusted the Father through the testings of the enemy in the wilderness. That met the power of Satan and sickness through all His earthly ministry with calm reliance upon His Father and victory over all power of the enemy. That stood at the grave of Lazarus and said, "I knew that you always hear me" (John 11:42a), "Lazarus, come out!" (11:43). That even upon the cross would say, "Father, into your hands I commit my spirit" (Luke 23:46). And afterwards could claim and promise to His disciples all the glories of His coming kingdom and the blessings of the gospel dispensation!

It is the same Christ who lives in us and inspires us with the faith of the Son of God, for our conflicts, testimonies and victories. He who says to us, "Have faith in God" (Mark 11:22) will not fail to impart it if we will receive Him and trust Him, and will enable us so to stand in all the hard places of our Christian lives, that as He is, so shall we be.

In our joy, we are filled with His gladness. The life of Christ was one of joy. Even in the darkest trials He often rejoiced in spirit. He had the inner and upper fountains of His Father's joy and love, and while He knew the depths of pain as no other spirit ever did, yet as is ever the case the pendulum touched both extremes. He also knew the heights of joy with equal intensity.

If we are filled with Christ we will have His joy in us and He has said it will be full. We won't have the hilarity of the world, and men may be unable to understand our happiness, but our deepest spirit will be filled with gladness and able to rejoice in the Lord when there is nothing else to light up the midnight of trouble.

In our love we may be even as He. Indeed in no other way can we meet the law of love and the demands and tests of Christian life except by His indwelling and the shedding abroad of His love in our hearts. But this He is willing to do if we are willing to stand in His love wherever He places us, and we will be able to pass triumphantly through every testing, perhaps with keen suffering, but without disobedience or sin and ever say, "But thanks be to God, who always leads us in triumphal procession in Christ" (2 Corinthians 2:14). "No, in all these things we are more than conquerors through him who loved us" (Romans 8:37).

In His glory we shall be like Him. "I have given them the glory that you gave me, that they may be one as we are one" (John 17:22).

When Joseph rose from a prison to a throne his greatest joy was to share his glory with his father and his father's house. Even when we receive a great blessing we long to share it with those we love.

So our precious Lord is not sitting amid the glories of heaven for His own delight as the ages go by. He is busy preparing our mansions and our crowns, and it will be His sublimest joy some day to open to us the vision of all He has been preparing for us during the years that we are suffering for Him below, and sometimes wondering if He had ceased to love us. Oh, how we shall fall at His feet in wonder and transport, and almost feel ashamed to take the crowns that He will place upon our heads!

That will be a happy day for us. But sometimes I think that it will be a happier day for Him, as He finds in our joy the consummation of His.

"What we will be has not yet been made known. But we know that when he appears, we shall be like him, for we shall see him as he is" (1 John 3:2), "because in this world we are like him" (4:17).

CHAPTER 7

Legacy in Verse

Simpson used verse as well as prose to express his understanding of God. The six poems that follow are only a small sample of his poetry. A larger collection can be found in *Songs of the Spirit* and *Hymns of the Christian Life*, the latter of these books is still in print and is published by Christian Publications.

Dr. Simpson believed and taught that to be "wholly sanctified" one first must grow tired of his failures and "look to Jesus." Jesus alone can meet man's deep needs. As the true seeker after God looks to Jesus, his prayer will be "search me, O God . . . and lead me in the way everlasting." As God reveals His will, the seeker will obey God and then will "get somewhere"—the place of sanctification—in his Christian life.

As the seeker continues to follow God, he will conclude that God "Himself" is total satisfaction, "Jesus Only," the exultant message and fulfilling "My Trust," the motivation of service.

Look to Jesus

Are you looking at your sins and failures?
   Look to Jesus.
Are you seeking to be saved by trying?
   Look to Jesus.
One sight of Him is worth a thousand tears,
One word from Him will banish all your fears,
One smile from Him, oh, how it helps and
     cheers,
   Look away to Jesus.

Are you looking at your grief and sorrow?
   Look to Jesus.
Are you anxious for the coming morrow?
   Look to Jesus.
One sight of Him will melt your clouds away,
One word from Him will turn your night to day,
One smile from Him illumine all your way,
   Look away to Jesus.

Has the vision of the world defiled you?
   Look to Jesus.
Has some smiling face of clay beguiled you?
   Look to Jesus.
One look at Him, and earth no more can charm,
One word from Him, and naught can e'er alarm,
One smile from Him will Satan's wiles disarm,
   Look away to Jesus.

Are you looking at your heart for feeling?
   Look to Jesus.

Are you looking for some sign of healing?
    Look to Jesus.
Look out, not in, and stop your vain repining,
Look past the cloud and see the silver lining,
He is your Sun and He is ever shining,
    Look away to Jesus.

Are you looking at the people round you?
    Look to Jesus.
Do the things that sometimes come astound you?
    Look to Jesus.
Look unto Him, for none but He can guide,
Look unto Him, no matter what betide,
Look unto Him, He always is beside,
    Look away to Jesus.

Search Me, O God

Search me, O God, search me and know my
        heart;
    Try me and prove me in the hidden part;
Cleanse me and make me holy, as Thou art,
    And lead me in the way everlasting.

Thou are the same today and yesterday:
    Oh, make Thy life in me the same alway.
Take from my heart the things that pass away;
    Lead, lead me in the way everlasting.

Take my poor heart and only let me love
    The things that always shall abiding prove.

Bind all my heartstrings to the world above,
  And lead me in the way everlasting.

Help me to lay my treasures up on high;
  Teach me to seek my future in the sky;
Give me my portion yonder by and by—
  And lead me in the way everlasting.

Oh, let my work abide the testing day
  That shall consume the stubble and the hay;
Oh, build my house upon the rock I pray—
  And lead me in the way everlasting.

Refrain:
Lead me, lead me, lead me in the way everlasting;
  Keep me from the things that wither and decay;
Give to me the things that cannot pass away—
  And lead me in the way everlasting.

Get Somewhere

Are you groping for a blessing,
  Never getting there?
Listen to a word in season,
  Get somewhere.

Are you struggling for salvation
  By your anxious prayer?
Stop your struggling, simply trust, and—
  Get somewhere.

Are you worn and heavy laden,
    Pressed with many a care?
Cast your burden on the Lord, and—
    Get somewhere.

Would you know the Great Physician
    Who your sickness bare?
Simply take Him at His word, and—
    Get somewhere.

Does the answer seem to linger
    To your earnest prayer?
Turn your praying into praise, and—
    Get somewhere.

Are you looking for your mission,
    What to do and dare?
Cease your dreaming, start at something—
    Get somewhere.

You will never know His fullness
    Till you boldly dare
To commit your all to Him, and—
    Get somewhere.

All your efforts are but building
    Castles in the air
Till you answer yes to God, and—
    Get somewhere.

Himself

Once it was the blessing,
    Now it is the Lord;
Once it was the feeling,
    Now it is His Word;
Once His gifts I wanted,
    Now the Giver own;
Once I sought for healing,
    Now Himself alone.

Once 'twas painful trying,
    Now 'tis perfect trust;
Once a half salvation,
    Now the uttermost;
Once 'twas ceaseless holding,
    Now he holds me fast;
Once 'twas constant drifting,
    Now my anchor's cast.

Once 'twas busy planning,
    Now 'tis trustful prayer;
Once 'twas anxious caring,
    Now He has the care;
Once 'twas what I wanted,
    Now what Jesus says;
Once 'twas constant asking,
    Now 'tis ceaseless praise.

Once it was my working,
    His it hence shall be;
Once I tried to use Him,
    Now He uses me;

Once the power I wanted,
  Now the Mighty One;
Once for self I labored,
  Now for Him alone.

Once I hoped in Jesus,
  Now I know He's mine;
Once my lamps were dying,
  Now they brightly shine;
Once for death I waited,
  Now His coming hail,
And my hopes are anchored,
  Safe within the vail.

Jesus Only

Jesus only is our Message,
  Jesus all our theme shall be;
We will lift up Jesus ever,
  Jesus only will we see.

Jesus only is our Savior,
  All our guilt He bore away,
All our righteousness, He gives us,
  All our strength from day to day.

Jesus is our Sanctifier,
  Cleansing us from self and sin,
And with all His Spirit's fullness
  Filling all our hearts within.

Jesus only is our Healer,
  All our sicknesses He bare,
And His risen life and fullness
  All His members still may share.
Jesus only is our Power,
  His the gift of Pentecost;
Jesus, breathe Thy power upon us,
  Fill us with the Holy Ghost.

And for Jesus we are waiting,
  Listening for the Advent Call;
But 'twill still be Jesus only,
  Jesus ever, all in all.

Jesus only! Jesus ever!
  Jesus All in all we sing!
Savior, Sanctifier, Healer,
  Glorious Lord, and Coming King!

My Trust

Lord, Thou hast given to me a trust,
  A high and holy dispensation,
To tell the world, and tell I must,
  The story of Thy great salvation.

Thou might'st have sent from heav'n above
  Angelic hosts to tell the story,
But in Thy condescending love,
  On men Thou hast conferred the glory.

Thou hast commanded us to go,
    Oh, never let our hearts betray Thee;
And thou hast left an awful woe,
    On all who lightly disobey Thee.

Oh, let us feel and fear that woe,
    As we would guard our own salvation,
And let us answer to that "go"
    As witnesses in every nation.

We are all debtors to our race;
    God holds us bound to one another;
The gifts and blessings of His grace
    Were given thee to give thy brother.

We owe to every child of sin
    One chance, at least, for hope of heaven,
Oh, by the love that brought us in,
    Let help and hope to them be given!

Refrain:
Let me be faithful to my trust,
    Telling the world the story;
Press on my heart the woe;
    Put in my feet the go;
Let me be faithful to my trust,
    And use me for Thy glory.

Other books by A.B. Simpson